Merce Cunningham's Events: Key Concepts

EVENT/FINAL

PALAISEAU

1 Dec 82

1' overture

Jigs

Scram s/w
f/l
duet
2 m
lines

ch St. solo LFB
floor duet
solo CK
trio JL-CAK-RR
solo MW
Q4 B
pullout duet

X currents

Scram LF
H

ch St.: Q$_5$ B
Solo LB
arm duet CK-CAK
trio HB-NG-LF
solo RS

Numbers

ch. St.
leg duet CK-HB
AG-LF

Scram: statues
3 men
dance

Jigs

MC

Finale

Claire Bishop

Merce Cunningham's Events: Key Concepts

Verlag der Buchhandlung
Walther und Franz König, Köln

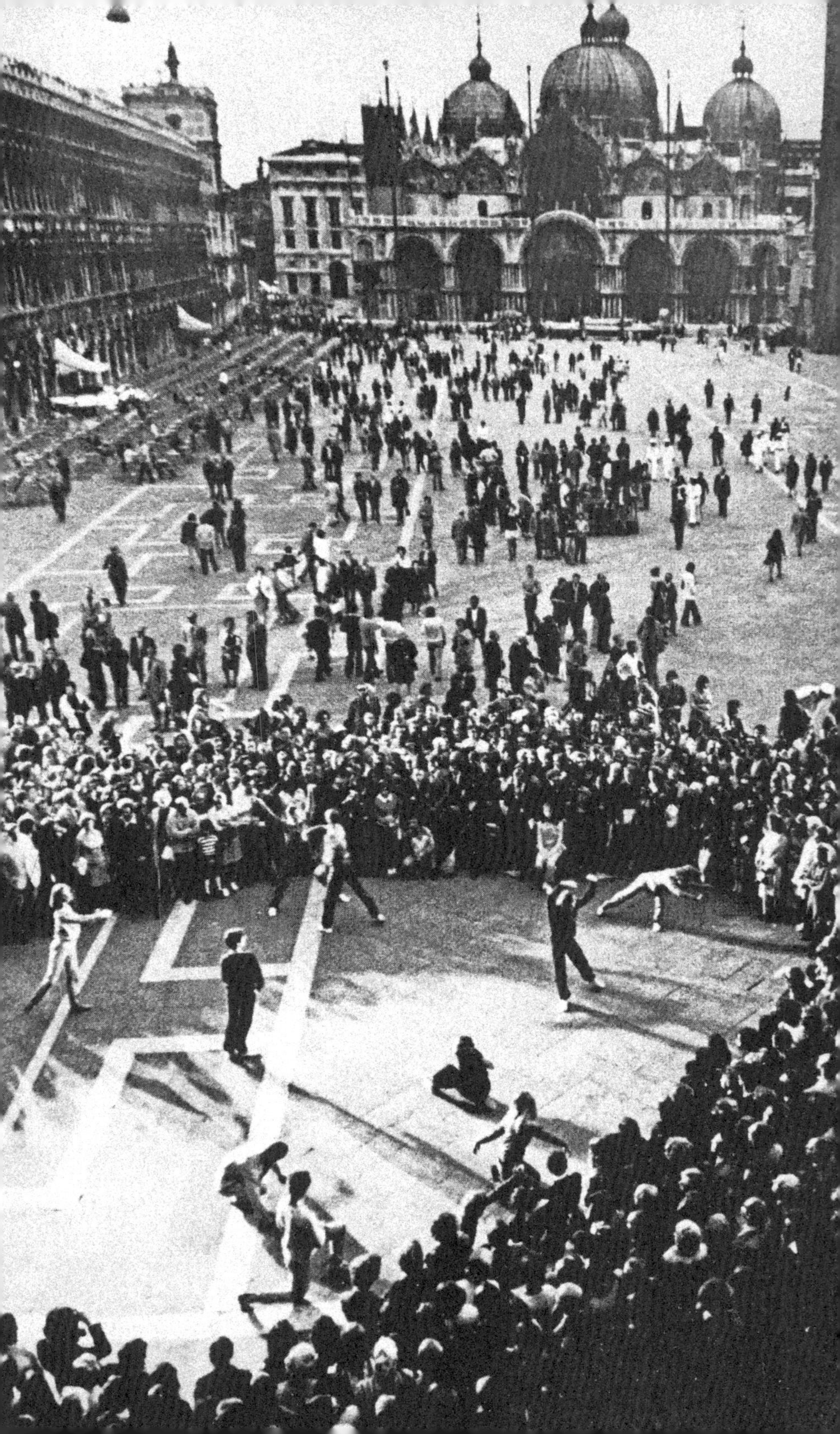

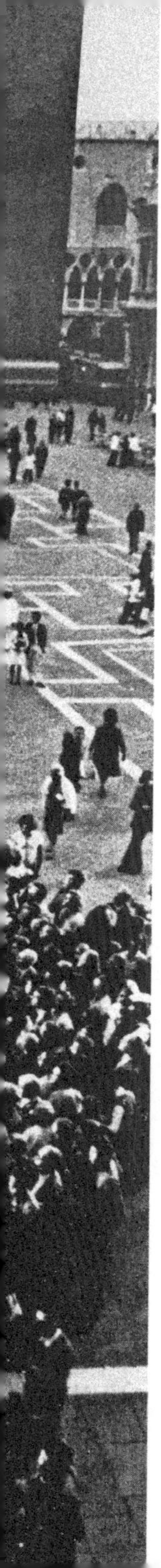

CONTENTS

Total reading time: 89'13

Previous spreads Order for Event #322, Centre d'Action Culturelle Acte, Palaiseau, France, 1 December 1982. Event #44, Piazza San Marco, Venice, 14 September 1972. Photo: James Klosty.

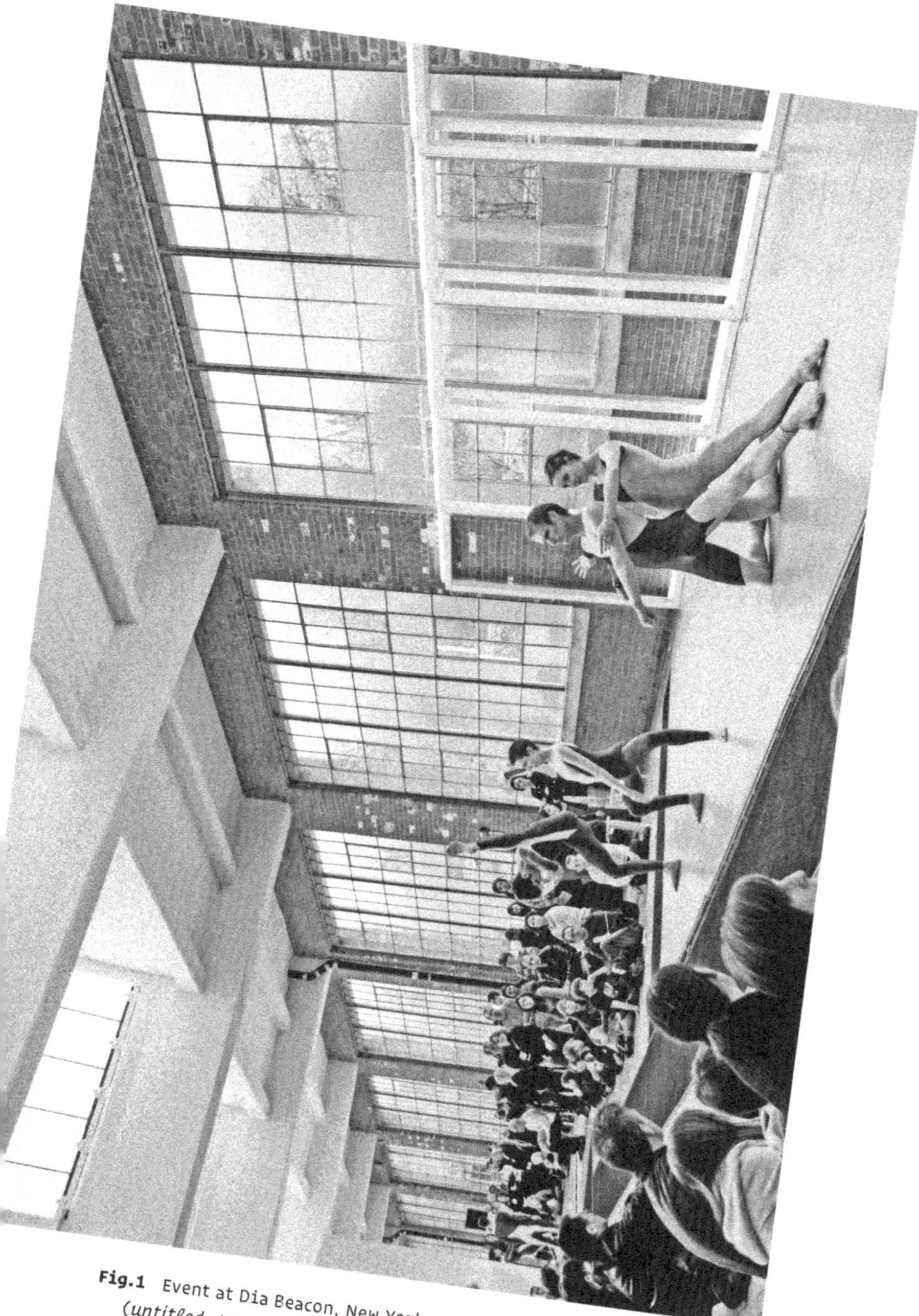

Fig.1 Event at Dia Beacon, New York, 2009. Sculpture by Dan Flavin (*untitled*, 1970). As part of the company's two-year residency at Dia Beacon, fourteen Events were performed in the galleries between 2007 and 2009. Photo: Anna Finke.

Prelude

While artists, curators, and art critics formed a dedicated audience for the choreographer Merce Cunningham (1909–2009) long before he received public acclaim—in part because of his close working relationships with Robert Rauschenberg, Jasper Johns, and other noted artists of the 1950s and 1960s—mainstream audiences and even dance reviewers often seem to have found his work challenging, even alienating. This seems to have been especially true of one category of Cunningham's performances, known as "Events," which he began in 1964. These differed from conventional evening presentations of dance, in which two or three complete pieces are separated by an intermission. Events, by contrast, comprised excerpts from Cunningham's repertory, parts of works in progress, and new Event-specific material—none of which was itemized on the program—and lasted ninety minutes without a break[1]. The order of excerpts changed each time, as did the musical accompaniment, which was performed live by a composer or musician. Sets, if they were used at all, also varied on each occasion, as did the costumes and lighting. Each Event was numbered, and never repeated.

Reviewers in the 1970s regularly mention the audience's difficulty at staying focused throughout such a lengthy duration of non-narrative dance without the relief of an intermission, and complain about the Events' apparent lack of structure. In 1971, Event #26 was described as "maddeningly

1. For a brief period from 1974 to 1976, the dances from which the excerpts were taken were listed in programs for Events at Westbeth, Cunningham's studio, but this practice was not continued.

 incomprehensible."[2] In 1972, "Cunningham has in all these years not learned how fully to capture the audience's attention. Again and again cultivated boredom sets in."[3] In 1973, "There was more restlessness, more audience irritation, more walking-out than I've ever seen at a Cunningham concert," reported *Dance Magazine*: "About half-way through [...], a large portion of the audience has had it. There's a large, loud walkout from the balcony (these people—many of them blacks from the neighborhood—are more than bored; they're mad)."[4] In 1975, the audience moved "out to the bathroom, for a smoke, or to leave permanently as they couldn't take the 'bleacher butt ache.'"[5] In 1976: "Ninety minutes, uninterrupted, is a sizeable chunk of choreographic time. It is long enough to seem an eternity. It is also long enough to prevent one from thinking in terms of beginning, middle, and end... [Events] are all middle."[6] This last review, by former *New York Times* dance critic Jack Anderson, goes furthest in a sceptical reading of Cunningham's Events: "There is often nothing—or very little—that one can say about them."[7]

Indeed, very little has been written about the Events. Yet by the time of Cunningham's death in 2009, more than eight hundred had been presented—effectively constituting a shadow practice that ran alongside his repertory productions for over four decades. In what follows, I want to argue that there is in fact a great deal to say about the Events—the focus just needs to shift from their content to their context, from choreographic form to conceptual format. Further, the Events provide an ideal lens for tracing the company's history, exploring (and demystifying) the central concepts of Cunningham's work, and observing the way in which material constraints tempered artistic creativity for choreographers in the second half of the twentieth century.

My starting point for this research was an interest in historicizing the recent trend for presenting dance in museums and galleries, for which Cunningham's Events seemed to be an important precursor.[8] Yet I quickly learned that museums were far from the only sites for Events; they simply have an outsize presence due to their photographic documentation, which is far more distinctive and numerous than that of Events in theatres **[Fig.1, Fig.2]**. This book nevertheless addresses the Events from the perspective of art history. This emphasis reflects my disciplinary bias: questions of

2. Jerry Klein, "Event No. 26 Leaves Audience Chewing, Bored, Wondering," *The Journal Star* (Peoria), March 5, 1971.

3. Reinhard Beuth, "The Lonely Avantgardist: Merce Cunningham and his Company in Düsseldorf," *Düsseldorfer Nachrichten*, October 6, 1972, n.p., original in Merce Cunningham Dance Foundation Inc. Records, Additions, (S)*MGZMD 351, box 255, folder 2, Jerome Robbins Dance Division, NYPLPA. All subsequent references to the Merce Cunningham Dance Foundation Inc. Records will state just the call number, box and folder. The original German reads: "Doch Cunningham hat es in all den Jahren nicht gelernt, das Publikum fest bei der Stange zu halten. Immer wieder breitet sich gepflegte Langweile aus." (Translation: Flora Brandl.)

4. Robb Baker, "Merce Cunningham and Dance Company," *Dance Magazine*, June 1973, n.p.; Merce Cunningham Dance Foundation Inc. Records, Additions, (S)*MGZMD 351, box 255, folder 3. This is a rare review that mentions the racial demographics of Cunningham's predominantly white audiences. Baker notes that in response to the walkout there was "horrified shushing," and the atmosphere became "increasingly tense," but there was "the usual standing ovation from the regular Cunningham fans." The characterization of (white) audiences as cultivatedly bored and Black audience members getting angry, while reductive and clichéd, nevertheless points to the limits of Cunningham's claim to universalizing neutrality (discussed below).

5. Francine Piggot, "Merce! An event," unidentified newspaper, April 24, 1975, n.p. Merce Cunningham Dance Foundation Inc. Records, Additions, (S)*MGZMD 351, box 255, folder 4.

6. Jack Anderson, "Dances about Everything and Dances about Some Things", *Ballet Review*, vol. 5, no. 4, 1976, p.58, p.60. Cunningham's repertory works of this period elicited similar responses: early press cuttings regularly note people walking out of performances (e.g., at a Boston performance of *Winterbranch*, reported in the *New York Times*, 11 November 1974). Dancer Carolyn Brown notes that *Landrover* (1972), at sixty minutes, with its minimal music and no décor, "challenged concentration, eliciting complaints of boredom." Brown, *Chance and Circumstance: Twenty Years with Cage and Cunningham*, NY: Alfred Knopf, 2007, p. 580.

7. Anderson, "Dances about Everything and Dances about Some Things," pp.56–60.

8. Museums and galleries began to program dance exhibitions in the late 2000s. For a brief history of this, see chapter two of my *Disordered Attention: How We Look at Art and Performance Today* (London: Verso, forthcoming).

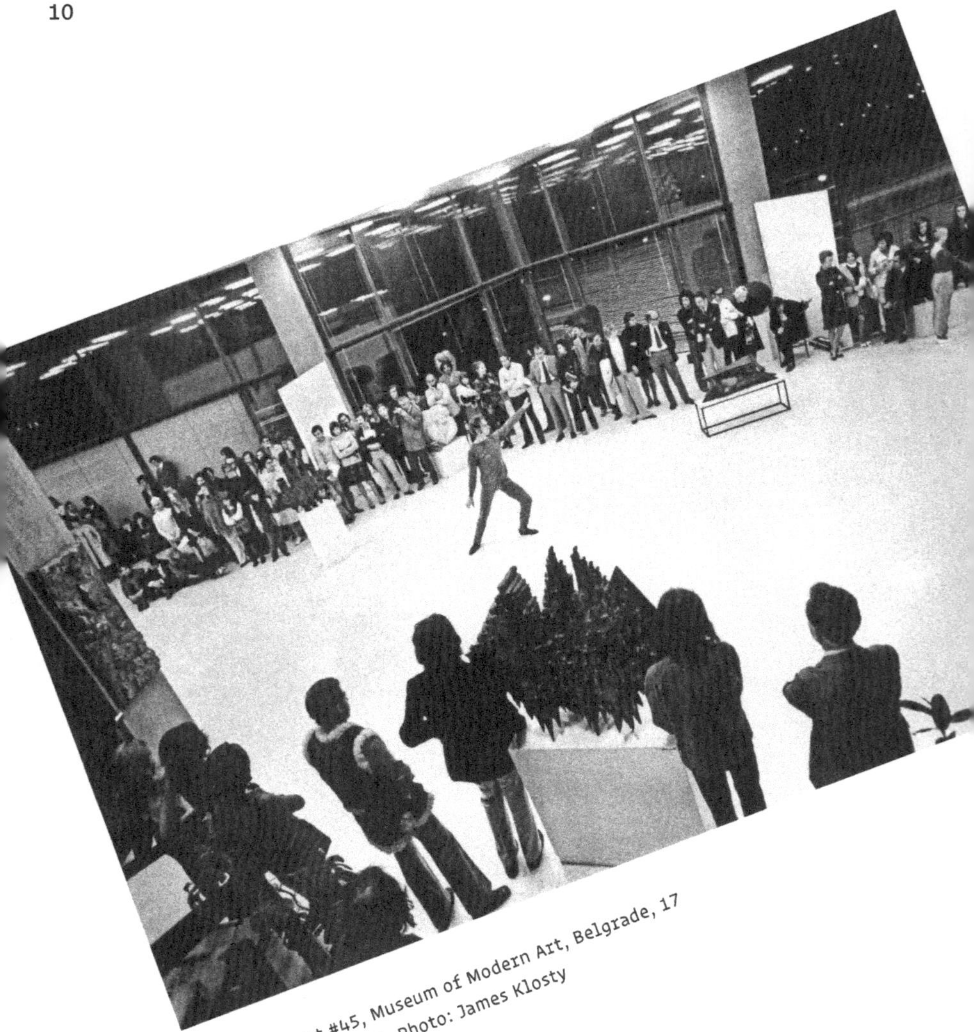

Fig.2 Event #45, Museum of Modern Art, Belgrade, 17 September 1972. Photo: James Klosty

10. Cunningham began his dance training aged twelve with Mrs Maude Barrett in Centralia, Washington, learning tap, waltz and vaudeville; he subsequently studied to be an actor at the Cornish School (where he met John Cage, who was faculty), and dance at Mills College, where he was spotted by Martha Graham, who cast him in works from 1939 to 1944. In 1944 he began working as an independent choreographer and collaborating with Cage, his lifelong partner.

9. For an analysis of Cunningham's work that pays meticulous attention to movement, I refer readers to Carrie Noland's excellent study *Merce Cunningham: After the Arbitrary*, Chicago, IL: Chicago University Press, 2019.

context, site, spectatorship, and institutions are ongoing preoccupations, rather than an analysis of choreographic movement.[9] The Events benefit from an art-historical optic because they emerge as much from a downtown experimental art milieu as from Cunningham's idiosyncratic background with Mrs Barrett, Martha Graham, and at Black Mountain College.[10] They offer incisive contributions to debates in art of the 1960s and 1970s to which his work was adjacent: issues of attention, technology, collaboration, duration, and recombination. With many of these concepts, I will argue, Cunningham is cautiously transitional, looking backwards as much as forwards.

This book tries to activate a materialist field of analysis for the Events, conjoining concrete matters of site, context, and unionization to conceptual issues of composition, collaboration, and legacy. The first section introduces the practicalities of Event production, which I use to chart a history of their development from Vienna in 1964 to New York in 2011, when crowds poured into the cavernous Park Avenue Armory for the final nights of the "legacy tour."[11] I then turn to Cunningham's decentralization of stage space and argue that his understanding of spectatorship was one of "choosing channels." From here, I show how the Events place pressure on, and even dismantle, conventional readings of Cunningham's work—especially the now overfamiliar concepts of chance, collage, and collaboration. Further sections focus on practical questions of corporate funding and unionization, and the question of how to judge the Events in light of Cunningham's claims for freedom (of spectatorship, of collaboration, of meaning). At the close, I return to the question of dance in museums, and what the Events open up in terms of spectatorship and contemporary developments in choreography.

11. The final six Events, each fifty minutes long and performed on three stages, were assembled by Robert Swinston, former company dancer and long-time assistant to the choreographer. Swinston has also assembled most of the Events performed since Cunningham's death, which I will not be discussing in this book.

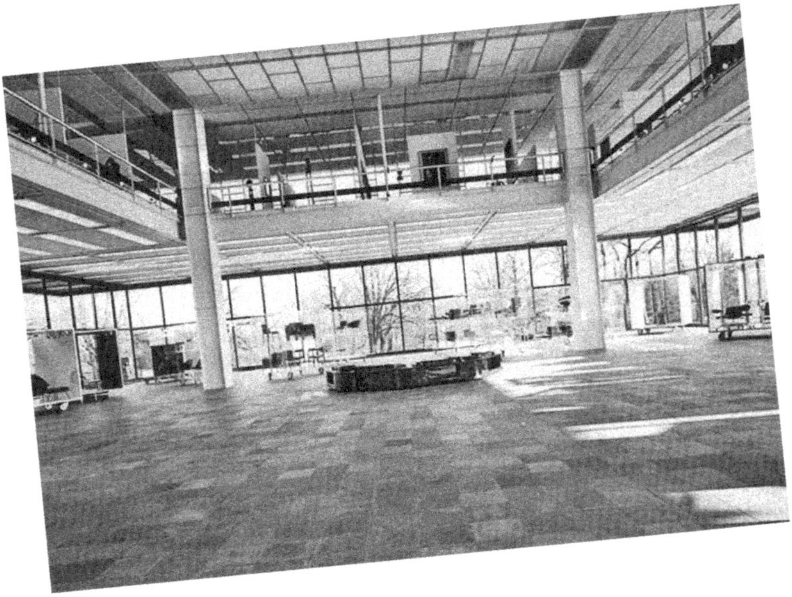

Fig.3 Interior of the Museum der 20. Jahrhunderts, Vienna, 1962. Architect: Karl Schwanzer. Built 1958–62. This is a view of the empty building; no photographs exist of Cunningham's first Event in this space on 24 June 1964. Photo: Lucca Chmel.

A quick note about how the Events are numbered. Company archivist David Vaughan made a list of all Events until the company dissolved in December 2011, but certain performances of Canfield (1969) in the early 1970s are listed as Events because Canfield has a variable structure and can last up to 75 minutes. Four Events in 1970 at the Fondation Maeght in the South of France were called Event I, Event II, Event III, and Event IV, but within the overall chronology they are Events 17 to 20. Museum Events and Gym Events were initially numbered separately. Starting in December 1971, Events were titled with an ongoing tally, but this system was abandoned by the end of May 1979. This publication works from the chronology of Events and MinEvents assembled by the current company archivist (and former dancer) Patricia Lent, who generously shared her research with me.

The first Event was created in June 1964 as a solution to the problem of how to present an evening of dance upon discovering there was no theatre at the venue in question, the Museum des 20. Jahrhunderts in Vienna. Today known as Belvedere 21, the museum is a modernist glass box without a demarcated performance area, making it impossible to stage two or three complete works separated by intermissions **[Fig.3]**. In response, Cunningham devised a program that recombined excerpts from his repertory dances into a continuous sequence lasting three hours, accompanied by John Cage's indeterminate score *Atlas Eclipticalis* (1961); Rauschenberg added electric light as daylight faded, and occasionally crossed the performance space "behung with the impedimenta of an umbrella fixer."[12] The audience reportedly met the work with "embarrassed silence," not knowing whether to applaud.[13] Cunningham, however, was sufficiently satisfied with the result to repeat the experiment three months later, performing Events #2 and #3 in what former dancer Carolyn Brown describes as a "mammoth gallery space" at the Moderna Museet in Stockholm.[14] Event #4 was held at another exhibition venue, Fondation Maeght in St Paul de Vence, and "took place all over the museum—in the galleries, in the sculpture court, and on the makeshift stage" at the end of the Giacometti sculpture garden.[15] **[Fig.4]**

12. Katherine S. Lobach, letter to Merce Cunningham, 1973, in Merce Cunningham Foundation Papers, (S)*MGZMD 196, box 22, folder 7. *Atlas Eclipticalis* was first used as the accompaniment to Cunningham's *Aeon* (1961). Lobach recalls that Cage's score provided "the impulse for an independent interpretation of sounds from plates, pans, wooden rollers, pots, and an assortment of noise makers, hand manipulated by musicians stationed in each corner of the room."

13. Lobach, letter to Merce Cunningham, 1973. Lobach was in the audience at the first Event in Vienna.

14. Carolyn Brown, *Chance and Circumstance*, p. 406. She describes the gallery having "an area three times as wide as the Metropolitan Opera House stage."

15. Carolyn Brown, *Chance and Circumstance*, p.477. Cunningham recalls dancing an excerpt of *Winterbranch* on the roof at Fondation Maeght, in Jacqueliine Lesschaeve, *The Dancer and the Dance: Merce Cunningham in conversation with Jacqueline Lesschaeve*, NY: Marion Boyers, 1985, p.176.

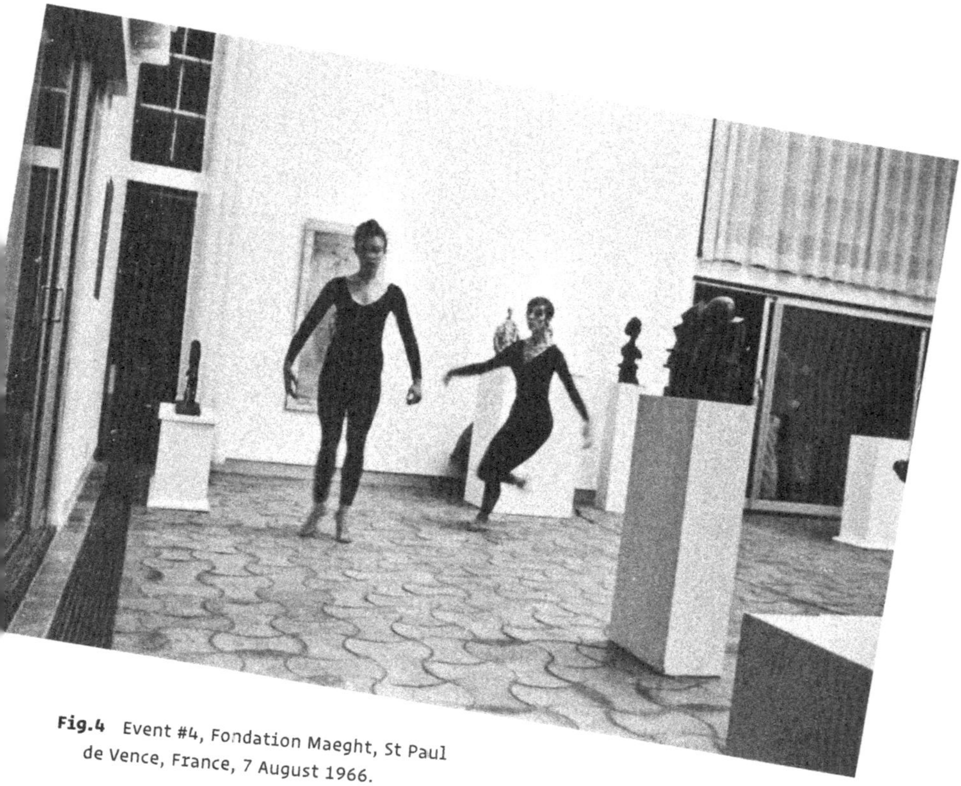

Fig.4 Event #4, Fondation Maeght, St Paul de Vence, France, 7 August 1966.

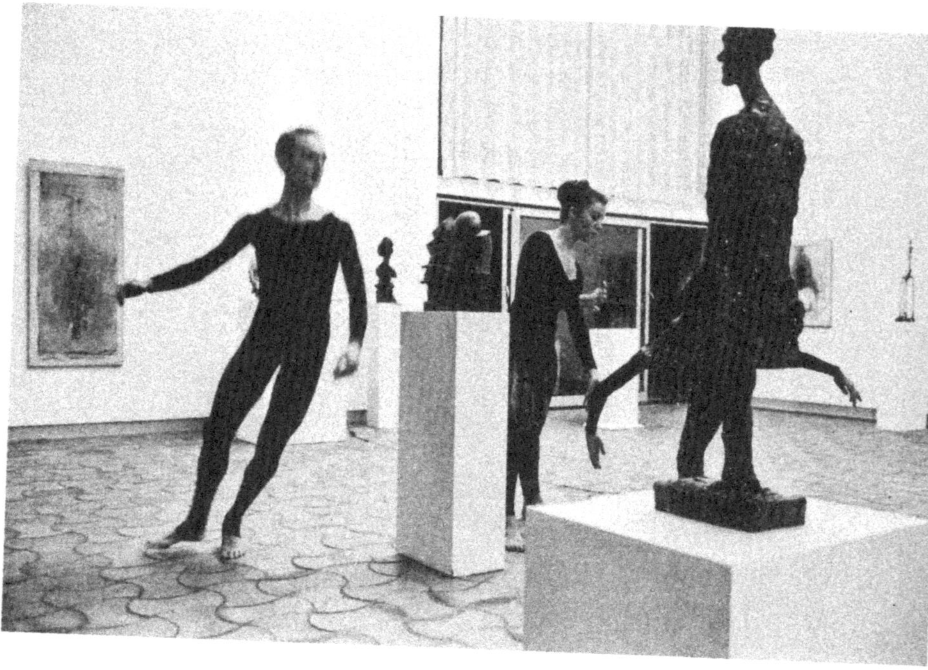

Back in New York, after returning from a six-month World Tour in November 1964, Cunningham's company was demoralized, in debt, and unpopular beyond a small cohort of experimental musicians and regular supporters in the art world. In 1966, the company was refused a federal subsidy for two European tours, despite Cunningham's two-decade career.[16] The grants awarded by the National Council on the Arts that year offer a telling indicator of his status: Cunningham, Alwin Nikolais, and Paul Taylor each received $5,000, compared to Anthony Tudor ($10,000), Jose Limon ($23,000), and Martha Graham—Cunningham's former employer—who received a whopping $181,000.[17] The company eventually received funding to appear in Mexico in advance of the 1968 Olympics and to tour South America (which turned out to be diplomatically fraught). In New York, few major venues were interested in presenting Cunningham's work; the company's 1969 shows at Brooklyn Academy of Music and the Billy Rose (now Nederlander) Theatre were notable exceptions.

16. The Dance Panel had first rejected Cunningham's application in 1955, arguing that his work was "too avantgarde and controversial." This opinion continued for another decade. See Naima Prevots, *Dance for Export: Cultural Diplomacy and the Cold War*, Wesleyan University Press, 1998, p.53.

17. Brown, *Chance and Circumstance*, p.466.

With little money or support, Cunningham turned to colleges and universities, personally writing to offer performances, lecture-demonstrations, dialogues, and workshops—receiving on average two replies for every fifty letters sent.[18] The company found themselves performing in college gymnasiums and basketball courts across the country, and so-called "Gym Events" became the go-to solution from Spring 1968 onwards. **[Fig.5]** There were rarely any sets, and lighting was just basic equipment that they brought with them in the company's Volkswagen bus.[19] Although Events were low-budget compared to full productions of the repertory, the company might drive two days to reach a remote college town, incurring costs for gas, meals, and motel rooms, which the performances did not recoup, while also losing rehearsal days and income from teaching classes.

18. Cunningham, transcript of the Dance Program Review and Guidelines Discussion at the 96th Meeting of the National Council of the Arts, 7 May 1988, in the Walker Art Center Archives, Box: WACA Folder Ref: RS 539.

19. Charles Atlas recalls that "we brought the lighting with us—say ten big lights and a lighting board." Interview with the author, New York, 14 March 2018.

In 1971, the company relocated to Westbeth, a subsidized housing complex for artists in the former Bell Laboratory

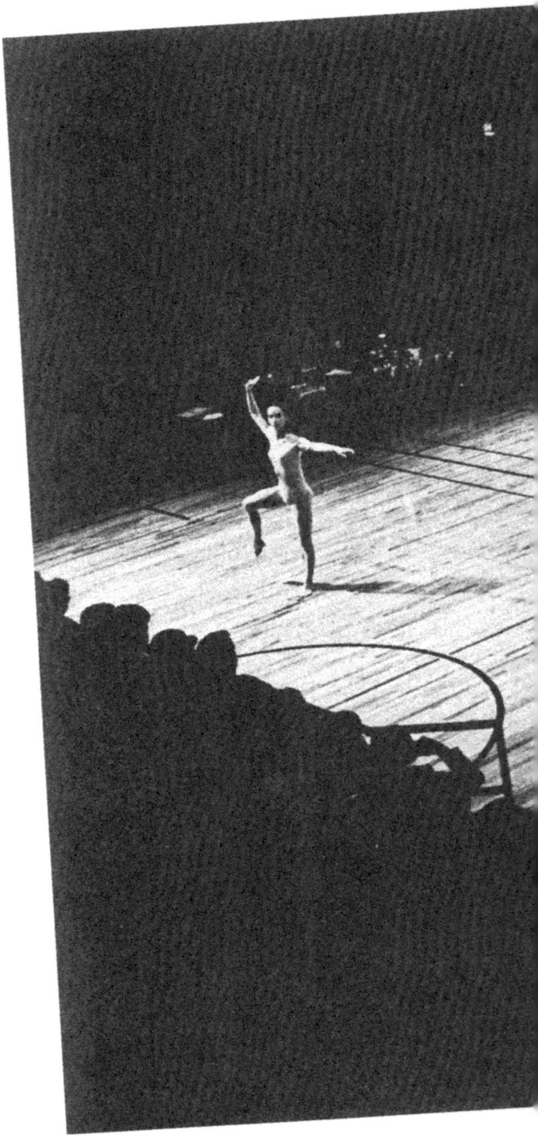

Fig.5 Event #21, Mills College, Oakland, CA, 20 January 1971. Photo: James Klosty

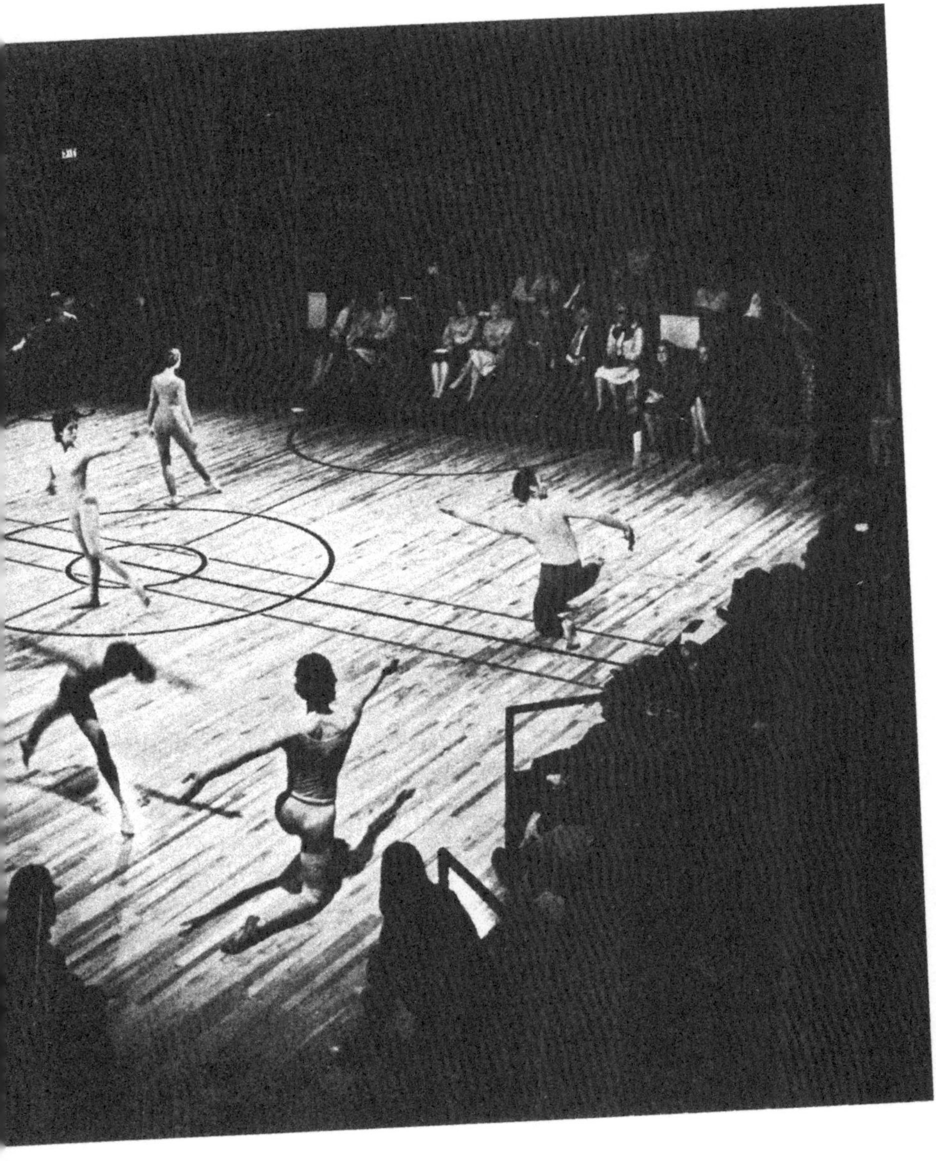

headquarters in lower Manhattan. This became the company's base for the remainder of its existence. The space was large enough to host performances, and in time the studio became home to a third of all Events performed during the 1970s.[20] The Westbeth Events became a way to present excerpts of new work to a small but sympathetic local audience. They also provided employment for the dancers, who were guaranteed twenty weeks of work after the company joined the union in 1969. Events took place at 8 or 9pm on consecutive weekend nights, for an audience of about seventy-five, some sitting on the floor only a few feet from the dancers.[21] Guest lists show attendees to be a combination of visual artists and musicians in Cunningham and Cage's milieu, students, and prospective donors who might support the company through these lean years. Dancer Valda Setterfield recalls that "it got very fashionable, and people were dying to get in. [...] Only Nureyev could show up and walk in without a ticket—it was more about potential donors and VIPs."[22] Indeed, reviewers in the mid-1970s frequently complained about the exclusivity of these performances, noting that the company effectively treated "public performances like private viewings," without any apparent interest in courting press coverage.[23]

Westbeth printed programs from around 1974–76 are unusual in listing the sources excerpted in the Events, which were usually a handful of recent repertory works and new pieces in the making. *Canfield* (1969), *Signals* (1970), *Loops* (1971), *TV Rerun* (1972), and *Landrover* (1972) are recurrent components—but not older works like *Aeon* (1961) and *Field Dances* (1963), which had featured in Event #1. **[Fig.6]** Throughout the mid-1970s, the Events were clearly a substitute for repertory performances; the only theatrical

20. In 1974, the company only performed twice outside Westbeth: two Events at BAM, and *Dialogue* at Walker Arts Center.

21. Composers in Cage's circle were invited to accompany the performances. Letters of invitation explain the audience situation (limited space, only 75 seats) and a duration of 60 to 75 minutes: "Set up space is limited, and unncessary personnel are a problem during the day as well as a confusion to our seating plans in the evening." Letter from Jean Rigg to composer Annea Lockwood, 11 February 1974, Merce Cunningham Dance Foundation Inc. Records, Additions, (S)*MGZMD 351, box 212, folder 5.

22. Valda Setterfield, interview with the author, New York, 14 March 2018.

23. Louise Pastore, "Joffrey's New Look, Pittsburgh's New Revival, and Cunningham's Special Events," *Dance Magazine*, May 1975, p.89. See also Jennifer Dunning, "Merce Cunningham: Audience As the Only Absolute," *Soho Weekly News*, January 1 1976, n.p. Jean Rigg's letters of invitation to composers (such as the one to Lockwood, above) each note that the Events are advertised in the *Village Voice*, the Center for New Music Calendar, and the music calendar of the *New York Times*. The suggested contribution was $3, but students with Theatre Development Fund vouchers could attend for $1.

CUNNINGHAM STUDIO AT WESTBETH
9:00 p.m. Friday, March 29

<u>home made synthesizer music with pitch-sensitive sensors</u>
by David Behrman

Participants: David Behrman and Katharine Morton

<u>Event #99</u> by Merce Cunningham

Dancers: Ellen Cornfield, Merce Cunningham, Meg Harper, Susana Hayman-Chaffey, Cathy Kerr, Chris Komar, Robert Kovich, Brynar Mehl, Charles Moulton, Julie Roess-Smith, Valda Setterfield

Event #99 is comprised of sections from <u>Landrover</u>, <u>Solo</u>, and <u>Summerspace</u>. This rehearsal and performance period has been made possible with support from the National Endowment for the Arts, the New York State Council on the Arts, and the Friends of Merce Cunningham.

There will be no intermission.

Lighting: Richard Nelson
Stage manager: Charles Atlas
Studio technical director: Nancy Golladay
House managers: Erika Bro and Gail Notarmuzi

Fig.6 Program for Event #99, Westbeth, New York, 29 March 1975. For a brief period, Event programs included a list of works excerpted, but did not indicate which sequences or the order in which they appeared—unlike the Event orders, discussed below.

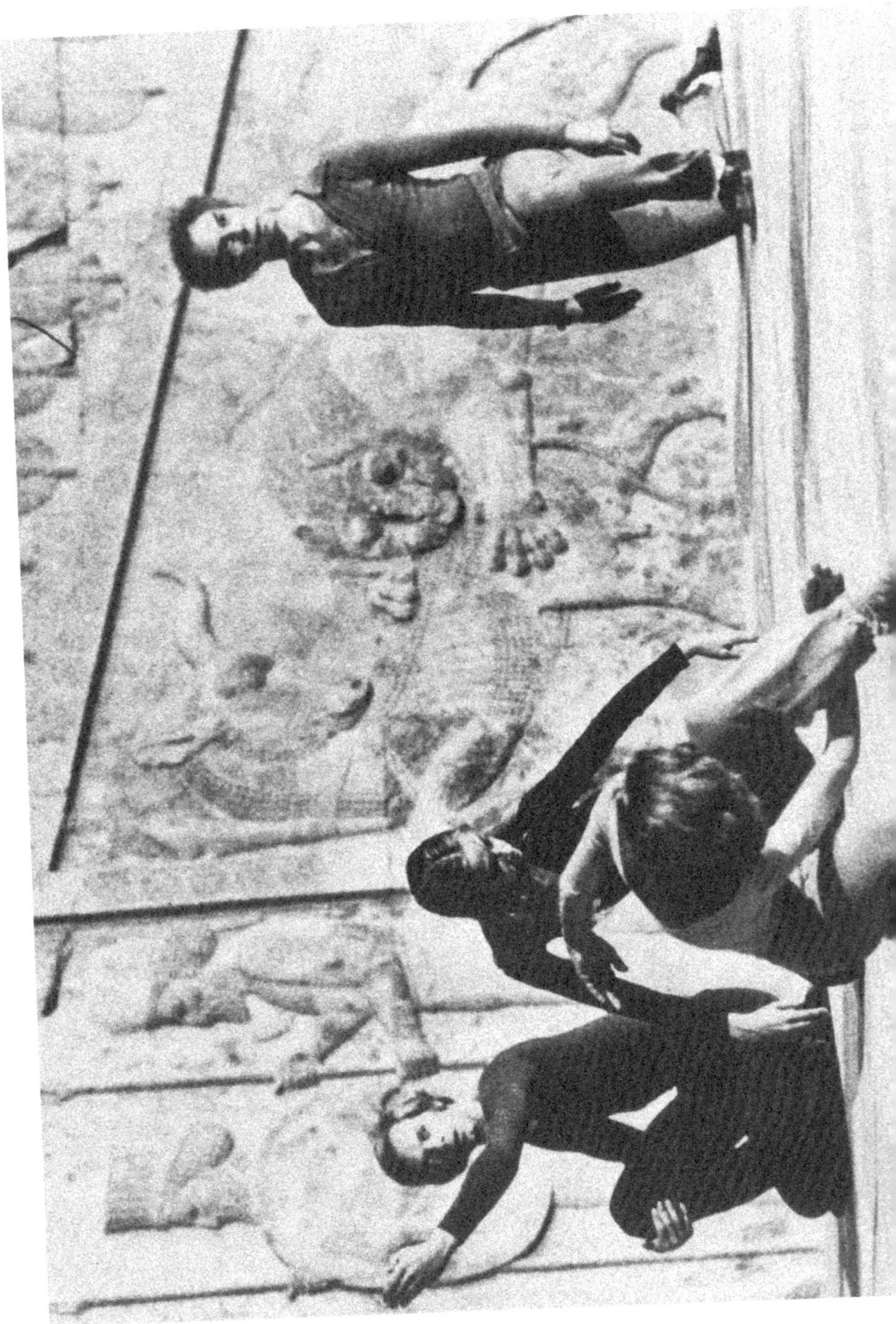

Fig.7 Event #43 ("Persepolis Event"), Persepolis, Iran, 8 September 1972. Photo: James Klosty.

presentations the company staged during these years continued to be in college and high school theatres, and in cities like Detroit and Minneapolis. On occasional tours to Europe, Events were staged outdoors in striking locations such as Piazza San Marco in Venice (1972), the ruins of Persepolis in Iran (also 1972), and ancient stone amphitheatres in Caesarea and Athens (both 1976). [Fig.7]

Between 1973 and 1975, Cunningham choreographed no new works, but began creating material specifically for Events rather than simply excerpting repertory.[24] This change resulted from the high turnover of dancers (especially men), culminating in Carolyn Brown's departure in 1972 after eighteen years with the company. Cunningham's earlier pieces had often relied on one or two star performers; he now devised new choreography that avoided this problem. In *Changing Steps*, first performed as part of an Event in 1973 (along with Cunningham's own solo *Loops*), every dancer is a soloist, innoculating Cunningham against the pain and frustration of star performers choosing to leave.[25] *TV Rerun*, a repertory work created the year of Brown's exit, fulfilled much the same function: in her words, "the dance was never jeopardized by the loss of any one dancer."[26] The traffic between full repertory production and Event was rarely two-way, however. Some (but not all) repertory could be fragmented into Events, while material composed for Events was rarely performed as a standalone work.[27]

24. My criteria for differentiating repertory and Event material is drawn from the performance chronologies created by company archivist Patricia Lent. *Loops* was first performed in the board room of the Museum of Modern Art (1971); its second performance was also at a museum, in the Composer's Showcase at the Whitney Museum of American Art. (1973). Thereafter it was integrated into Events. When shown as repertory, *Loops* was always presented alongside *Changing Steps*, with only very few late exceptions.

Over the course of the 1980s and 1990s, Cunningham became a cultural fixture rather than controversial vanguard, and the company performed more repertory works at theater venues. The company continued to present Events in mid-size theatres too small to accommodate full-scale productions, such as the Joyce Theatre (in New York), Palais Garnier (in Paris) and Jacob's Pillow (in Massachusetts). An Event tour, such as the European one of November 1982, or the Asian trip of January

25. Cunningham, in Lesschaeve, *The Dancer and the Dance*, p.154.

26. Brown, *Chance and Circumstance*, p.570.

27. *Changing Steps* is the exception: it went on to have an intermittent life as a repertory work (1975–83), and was filmed in 1988, but its primary home was within Events.

1984, enabled the company to perform in a wide range of venues without incurring extensive costs for transporting sets and costumes. Musicians, however, remained a priority: Cage and his entourage were always present.[28] Although Cunningham occasionally continued to perform Events in colleges, museums, and gyms, these venues were no longer regular features of company tours.

Back home, week-long runs of Events at the Joyce Theatre (1984, 1985, 1994, 1996) became a low-cost way to present work to a New York audience, with minimal rehearsal requirements. The Event order was arranged the day of the performance—in part to economize on time, and in part to sustain a certain intensity of focus in the dancers. After class in the morning, rehearsals began at 1pm for that evening's Event; Cunningham would read aloud the order, which the dancers jotted down. The company would then run through the program, concentrating not so much on the specific sequences (which were all well known to them) but the transitions and facings (that is, the direction of the dancer's body).[29] A change of facing could be disorienting for the dancer, but this interested Cunningham because it kept the performer on edge, exuding a heightened alertness.

As a way to keep older works alive without the expense of a full production, Events were pragmatic archives. Pieces were phased out of repertory, but slowly gained a new life as decontextualized sequences in Events. Ever practical, Cunningham found that Events also served an internal function, since they were a way to ensure that each generation of dancers became familiar with older material. By the late 1990s, certain works were always taught to the repertory understudy group (RUG), such as *Signals* and *Changing Steps*, so that dancers were partially equipped to perform Events upon promotion to the company.

28. "As we began to go on longer tours, and the economics of running a dance company took on Everest proportions, practicality pulled some of this [collaboration with visual artists] down. Getting freight and personnel around the work, not to speak of cost, was becoming uncertain enough to bring about new necessities. We began to give more Events in order to accommodate this present situation." Cunningham, 'Collaborating with Visual Artists' (1983), unpublished essay, https://www.mercecunningham.org/the-work/writings/collaborating-with-visual-artists/. Neil Greenberg recalls the French tour of 1982, in which "carting musicians around was a real priority, not sets. Hence Events. Taking Cage, Tudor, Kosugi, etc was a real financial priority for the company." Greenberg, interview with the author, New York, 8 March 2018.

29. Greenberg again: "There were never any major revisions. It was all about logistics—it was all really well thought out before hand [...] The sections were very rehearsed, and securely in the body, but the transitions were unknown." Greenberg, interview with the author, New York, 8 March 2018.

The rhetoric of uniqueness and individuality that had always been present in Cunningham's descriptions of the Events now became an explicit marketing tool. Each Event was claimed to be one-off, site-specific, and novel, thereby appealing to producers and programmers who could not afford a new commission.[30] A press release for the Joyce Theatre in 1984 sums it up: "Each night, the Event is different."[31] **[Fig.8]** The slippage between *uniqueness* (which is true of any performance) and *newness* (which implies

30. Cunningham described Events as "arranged for the particular stage upon which it will be given." See for example Cunningham, "Events," undated page, in Merce Cunningham Dance Foundation Inc. Records, (S)*MGZMD 196, box 16, folder 24.

31. Press release by Ellen Jacobs Associates for a nine-day series of Events at the Joyce Theatre, 1984. Merce Cunningham Dance Foundation Inc. Records, Additions, (S)*MGZMD 351, box 233, folder 11.

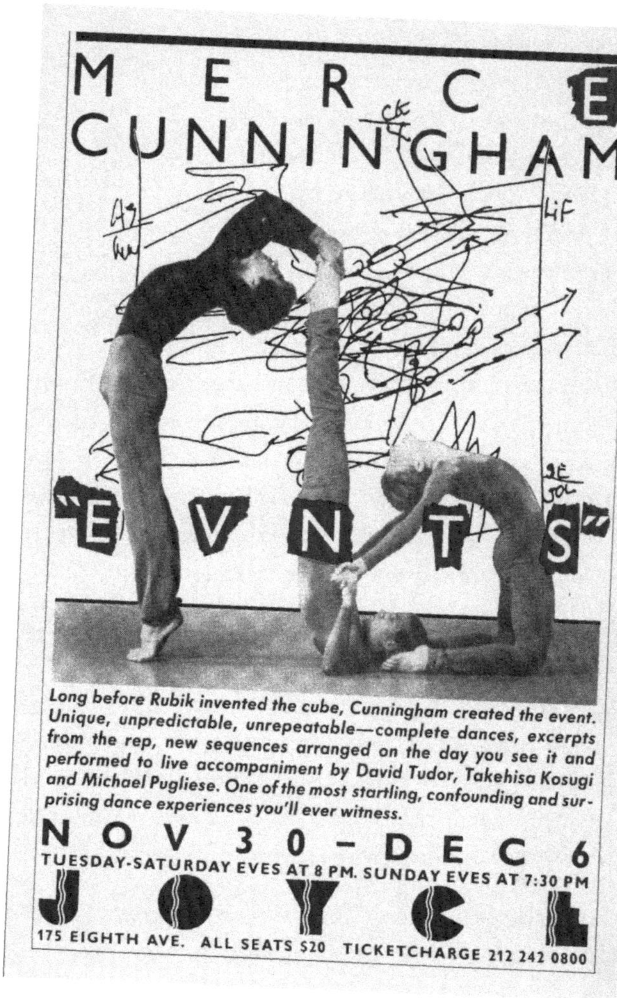

Fig.8 Merce Cunningham Dance Company poster from The Joyce, New York City, 1985. Note the adjectives: "Unique, unrepeatable, unpredictable."

more creative complexity) was exploited by venues to Cunningham's advantage. As time went on, Events enabled the choreographer to decline invitations to make new work when he had decreasing energy for such projects. When the Walker Art Center asked if they could commission Cunningham to make a new work to celebrate the tenth anniversary of the Sculpture Garden in 1998, for example, he replied that he could only provide an "event for the garden"—which curator Philip Bither admitted was "not exactly a new work."[32] The pressure to be delivering the "new" is a perennial condition of cultural funding, and the company expediently deployed Events as a way to navigate institutional desires and expectations.[33]

The new millennium was characterized by strategic sponsorships and collaborations, not least because the company was now larger than it had ever been (from five members in 1953 to eighteen by 2009).[34] The "AmEx Event" (2002) was underwritten by American Express, and took place at company headquarters in New York's financial district to celebrate the re-opening of the building after 9/11.[35] Dancers performed in an exhibition of portraits of card-holding celebrities (including Cunningham), photographed by Annie Leibovitz, which were displayed in seven mesh-like pods connected by a series of catwalks. **[Fig.9]** While the context was unsympathetic to say the least, it is a salutary reminder that Cunningham never fretted over the purity of a site. His attitude remained much as it had been in 1964:

> The space as given with impediment is the theatre, the impediment is not impediment but the landscape in which the event happens. A street of hard cement and oil stains, the sanctuary of a church, an art gallery complete with paintings on the walls and objects here and there. And no attempt is made to change it, or by screens, curtains or containers, to hint at some idea of a theatre.[36]

If anything, restrictions and limitations were perceived as generative, demanding a creative new solution. In the case of American

32. Memo from Philip Bither to Philippe Vergne, 4 March 1997, Walker Art Center Archive, Box: WACA Folder Ref: RS 539.

33. In 2004, Dance Umbrella commissioned Cunningham for a six-city UK tour. The first five venues hosted Events, in which different aspects of a new repertory work were premiered—choreography, design, lighting, costumes, and music. The whole production only came together at the last stop, Edinburgh, where *Views on Stage* (2004) received its "world premiere." Trevor Carlson, interview with the author, via Skype, 22 February 2018.

34. One such collaboration was *EyeSpace* (2006), originally proposed to Apple as the "iPod Event." The dance company hoped to receive one million dollars for the commission, and one million dollars per year to support the piece's tour. In the end, Apple didn't follow through with sponsorship, leaving the company to buy its own iPods. During *EyeSpace*, each member of the audience listens to Mikel Rouse's ambient score on an iPod shuffle; the sequence of the music is randomized, thereby individualizing each audience member's experience. *EyeSpace* was dropped from repertory in 2008–9. See Merce Cunningham Dance Foundation Inc. Records, Additions, (S)*MGZMD 351, box 214, folder 3.

35. AmEx's contribution of $120,000 for the commission left the dance company with a profit of $65,000. Minutes of the Board of Directors, 16 January 2003, in Merce Cunningham Dance Foundation Inc. Records, Additions, (S)*MGZMD 351, box 17, folder 1.

36. Cunningham, lecture draft for Hartford, CT, 19 March 1964, in Merce Cunningham Dance Foundation Inc. Records, Additions, (S)*MGZMD 351, box 29, folder 2, pp.11–12.

Fig.9 Contact sheet of photographs of the "AmEx Event," World Financial Center, New York, 18 December 2002. This was the first multi-stage Event. "Rewarding Lives" was the title of the exhibition within which the performance took place.

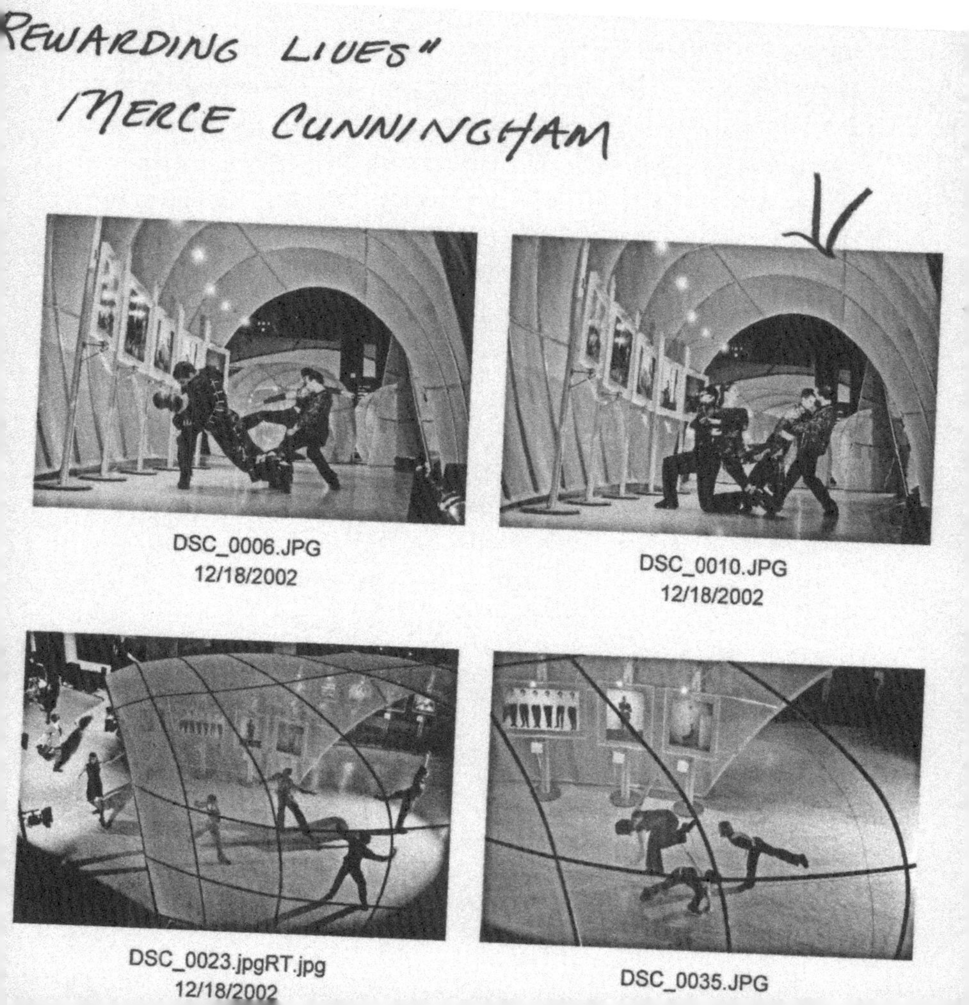

Express, it served as a motor of invention for splitting the Events across several stages simultaneously, which led to a reinvigoration of the Event form in the 2000s.

During Cunningham's final decade, the company made a return to museums, presenting multi-stage events at Tate Modern (2003), the Museo Reina Sofía (2009), and Dia Beacon (2009), among others. Because the area for dancing was now much smaller (especially in comparison to the gymnasiums and amphitheatres of the 1970s), excerpts tended to be solos, duets, and trios, rather than sequences involving the entire company. They were also correspondingly shorter—in the words of dancer Neil Greenberg, "little jewels, without the settings."[37] Art institutions offered a different type of strategic collaboration. The "Craneway Event" (2009), for example, held in a cavernous disused Ford plant in San Francisco, was documented in an eponymous 16mm film installation by the British artist Tacita Dean; her work is usually sold in an edition of three, one of which was donated to the dance company.[38]

Museums have come to be seen as central to the innovation of the Events—in part because the performances can (at least in theory) be seen from all sides, like sculpture, and in part because Cunningham's choreography, as dance historian Roger Copeland observes, "resembles the cool, ultra-clean, impersonal environment of the modern museum."[39] **[Fig.10, Fig.11]** Yet gymnasia, theatres, armories, and the studio at Westbeth were equally important to their development and transformation, while the outdoor performances best capture the ideas of adaptability and freedom within constraints that are central to the Events as a genre.

37. Neil Greenberg, interview with the author, New York, 8 March 2018.

38. Carlson recalls that "Craneway Event" satisfied the company's financial shortfall and even generated additional revenue for rehearsal weeks in New York, thanks to the support of moving image collector Pamela Kramlich. Carlson, interview with the author, via Skype, 14 December 2019.

39. Roger Copeland, "Merce Cunningham and the Politics of Perception" (1979), in Roger Copeland and Marshall Cohen (eds), *What is Dance? Readings in Theory and Criticism*, Oxford: Oxford University Press, 1983, p.318.

Fig.11

"Anniversary Event" at Tate Modern, London, November 2003. Dance Umbrella commissioned a series of eight Events to celebrate the festival's twenty-fifth anniversary and the company's fiftieth anniversary. The performances took place inside Olafur Eliasson's installation *The Weather Project* (2003), with live sound by Takehisa Kosugi. Photo: Robbie Jack.

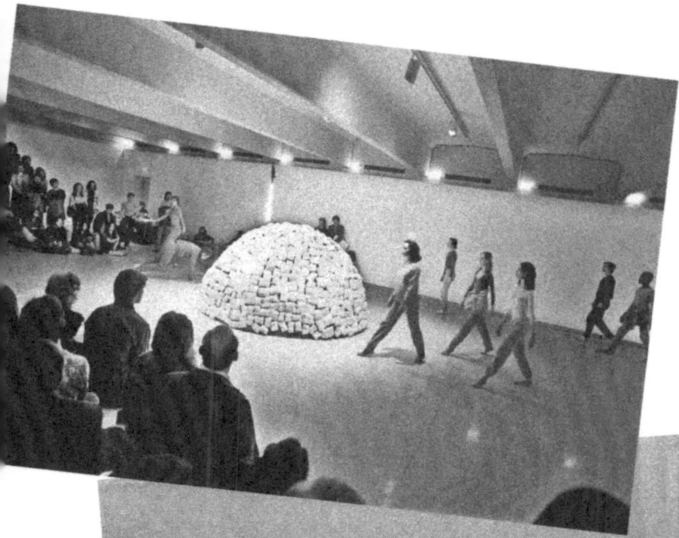

Fig.10 Event #32, Walker Art Center, Minneapolis, 12 March 1972. This Event was a full performance of *Canfield* (1969) in various galleries; this image shows *Fibonacci Igloo* (1972) by Mario Merz. Photo: James Klosty.

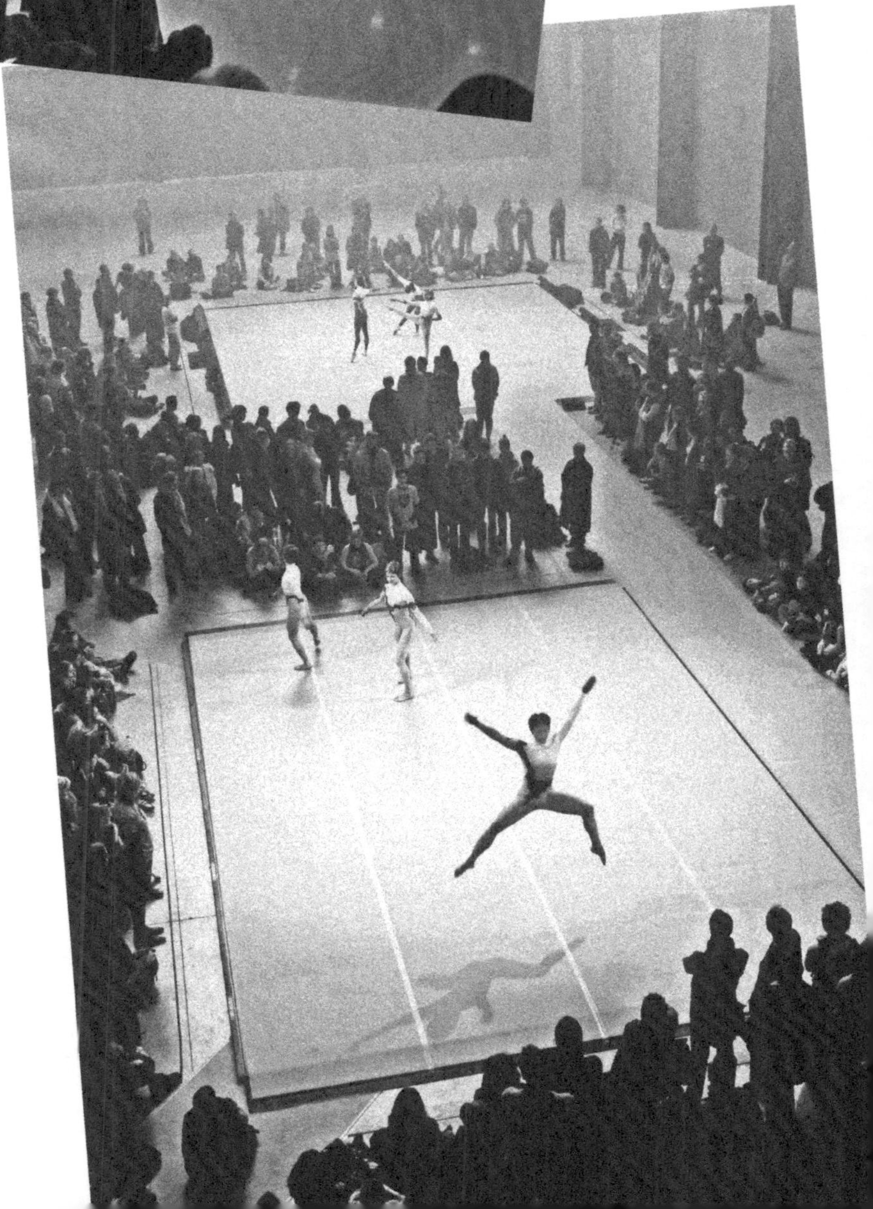

Cunningham is conventionally credited with two major shifts in the presentation of modern dance: decentering stage space and dehierarchizing the arrangement of dancers. Both innovations shift the performance from a frontal presentation to a multidirectional one. Since its origins at the French royal court of Louis XIV in the seventeenth century, ballet has organized activity onstage around clear focal points (a solo, a duet, a trio), supported by secondary dancers (the *corps de ballet*), all of whom face the audience. This legacy continued more or less uninterrupted into the twentieth century. Modern dancer Doris Humphrey, for example, in her choreographic manual from 1959, divides the stage into six "weak" and seven "strong" areas, and suggests that "the full impact of the body should be directed to the front wherever possible."[40] Cunningham, by contrast, frequently spoke of the need to reject two hundred years of proscenium staging, with its frontal organization of performance and consolidation of sightlines from royal box to perspectival vanishing point. In contrast, his choreography provided no single point of focus in group sequences, and performers might face in any direction, even turning their backs to the audience.

Cunningham's interest in multi-directional stage space is usually credited to John Cage's *Theatre Piece No. 1* at Black Mountain College in 1952. Made in collaboration with Cunningham, Rauschenberg, musician David Tudor, and two poets (MC Richards

40. Doris Humphrey, *The Art of Making Dances*, NY: Grove Press, 1959, p.82, p.85. She observes that dance is not like good sculpture, equally arresting from all angles; it is best seen from only one direction (p.90). For a good discussion of Cunningham's *Summerspace* as a rejection of this formal convention, see Noland, *Merce Cunningham: After the Arbitrary*, pp.48–52.

and Charles Olson), *Theatre Piece No. 1* combined music, dance, projected film, and poetry within timeframes established in advance by Cage. The audience was seated in four triangular blocks facing outward in different directions.[41] This mix of independent components in different media is often seen as similar to Cunningham's work, but was more radical in its dispersal of the audience's focus across four seating areas. The legacy of *Theater Piece No. 1* can best be seen in the happenings and other performances of the early 1960s. Cunningham's compositions, by contrast, occupy stage space in a more conventional manner, even while they gently pressure the frontality of this tradition.

41. No documentation of *Theatre Piece No.1* exists, only a later diagram of the action by Richards, frequently reproduced in discussions of the work. Firsthand accounts vary. For a synopsis, see Kenneth Silverman, *Begin Again: A Biography of John Cage*, Evanston, IL: Northwestern University Press, 2012, pp.115-116, and Ruth Erickson, "Chance Encounters: Theatre Piece No.1 and its Prehistory," in Helen Molesworth, ed., *Leap Before You Look: Black Mountain College, 1933-1957*, Boston: Institute of Contemporary Art, 2015, pp.298-301.

Another comparison can be made to choreographer Anna Halprin, who taught classes and hosted performers on an outdoor "dance deck," located in a redwood forest outside San Francisco. Cunningham lectured and performed there in 1957, and the deck is mentioned in several of his talks from the late 1950s. **[Fig.12]** He contrasted the openness of the dance deck with the proscenium

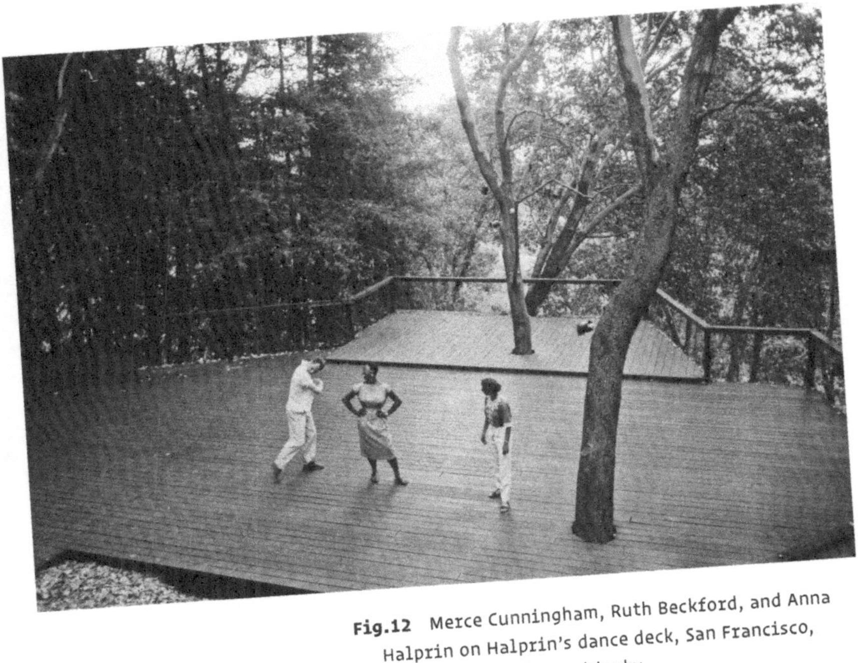

Fig.12 Merce Cunningham, Ruth Beckford, and Anna Halprin on Halprin's dance deck, San Francisco, 1957. Photo: Ted Streshinsky.

stage, "where the vision on both sides is limited, slightly like a horse with blinders."[42] On Halprin's deck, which was positioned on a slope jutting out into the woods, a dancer "does not always feel the necessity to face 'front' […] The audience can be seated all the way around." Since the area behind Halprin's deck is a forested slope, this may have been a misremembering; most photographs show the audience sitting on six wooden bleachers facing the stage.

42. Cunningham, Lecture-Demonstration, Taft Lecture Series/University of Illinois, 3 March 1959, p.6, Merce Cunningham Dance Foundation Inc. Records, Additions, (S)*MGZMD 351, box 29, folder 1.

Yet the experience of Halprin's deck seemed to have confirmed an approach to multi-sided composition that was already part of Cunningham's thinking in the 1950s. As early as 1952, *Suite by Chance* "was conceived to be seen from four sides and was presented so whenever possible. Any angle of vision was permissible, as in the streets."[43] The dancers in *Galaxy* (1956) similarly face all directions, not just front. This (theoretical) multi-sidedness existed in tension with the fact that most of Cunningham's repertory productions were presented in proscenium theaters where the audience was seated in front of the stage. Only Events in museums, gymnasia, and other nontraditional settings without fixed seating allowed the opportunity for viewing from multiple angles—even though audiences tended to remain seated in the same place for the duration of the work (as on Halprin's deck). Few Events actively encouraged viewers to see the performance from all four sides; the virtuosity of the dancers and the experimentalism of the music both tended to inhibit mobility and conversation.

43. Cunningham, in Arlene Croce, "An Interview with Merce Cunningham," *Ballet Review* vol.1, no.4, 1966, p.3.

Cunningham often quoted Albert Einstein's dictum that "there are no fixed points in space," and this is frequently invoked as shorthand to explain the choreographer's interest in a multi-directional occupation of the stage.[44] It's both a misunderstanding of the theory of relativity and a cherry-picked reference to Einstein.[45] The rest of Cunningham's lectures of the 1960s turn not to modern physics but to more readily graspable frameworks derived from music and technology. "We have thought to

44. Cunningham, Lecture-Demonstration for Bennington College, VT, 15 Nov 1961, n.p., in Merce Cunningham Dance Foundation Inc. Records, Additions, (S)*MGZMD 351, box 29, folder 1. See also Cunningham, lecture for Douglas College, New Brunswick, p.4; Lesschaeve, *The Dancer and the Dance*, p.18.

45. Einstein is discussing the relativity of *motion*, while Cunningham is talking about relativity of *location*.

look in one direction for hundreds of years now," he observes in a 1965 lecture, "but perhaps that will change with television, men in space, and automation."[46] In interviews and lectures throughout the 1960s (and even into the 1970s and 1980s), he regularly turn to these motifs as a way to describe the audience's dispersal of attention. He continually invokes the street as a non-hierarchical visual space in which people are seen from all sides. Television and space travel, meanwhile, construct the world as an immersive "field of attention" rather than as linear perspective:

46. Cunningham, Lecture draft, Foundation for Arts, Religion and Culture, Oct 1965, p.5. Merce Cunningham Dance Foundation Inc. Records, Additions, (S)*MGZMD 351, box 29, folder 2.

> The idea of a proscenium stage seems to me out of place now. A man floating in space, weightless, the other side of the moon, the earth from 275 miles up. These have all changed our angle of vision. We know now within us that we see, and are seen from all angles.[47]

47. Cunningham, Lecture draft for Douglas College, New Brunswick, 8 April 1965, p.4, in Merce Cunningham Dance Foundation Inc. Records, Additions, (S)*MGZMD 351, box 29, folder 2.

Although *field* was a term already deployed by Cage in the 1950s, Cunningham's usage owes more to media theorist Marshall McLuhan, who mobilizes the word to refer specifically to new modes of human perception.[48] In *The Gutenberg Galaxy* (1962), McLuhan makes characteristically sweeping assertions about the human internalization of technology—from cave paintings to symbolist poetry—culminating in the "total electric field culture of our time."[49] This "unified field of electric all-at-onceness," he enthuses, creates a global village of electronic simultaneity and interdependence that undoes the sensory division of labour synonymous with industrial modernity. McLuhan thus opposes the "field" to the linearity of factory production (rather than to the sight-lines of royal theatre) yet the contrast he draws is strikingly similar to Cunningham's rejection of perspective in favour of multi-centered stage space. McLuhan even prefaces his book by claiming it takes a "mosaic or field approach to

48. Cage's use of "field" was informed by his experience of new electronic sound technologies, especially magnetic tape. It denoted the world of every possible sound, rather than music traditionally understood as a system of scales and notes. The conventional opposition of sound/silence could thus be replaced by the electromagnetic model of field and continuity. Composition for Cage no longer began from the mind of the composer, but drew its materials from an acoustical "field" of possibilities. See Branden Joseph, "Chance, Indeterminacy, Multiplicity," in Julia Robinson (ed.), *The Anarchy of Silence: John Cage and Experimental Art*, Barcelona: MACBA, 2010, p.219.

49. Marshall McLuhan, *The Gutenberg Galaxy: The Making of Typographic Man*, Toronto: University of Toronto Press, (1962) 1966, p.29.

its problems," proceeding as a constellation or galaxy rather than as "a series of views of fixed relationships in space."[50] This phrase alone, with its subliminal echo of Einstein, would have caught Cunningham's eye.

50. McLuhan, *The Gutenberg Galaxy*, n.p. (page between the Table of Contents and page 1).

Cunningham was clearly familiar with McLuhan's ideas. In a 1966 interview, Cunningham says that he agrees with McLuhan's proposal that television and new media change patterns of logic, and shift composition from "linear to field."[51] Yet what he took from the media theorist was primarily the encouragement to use, as fully as possible, the technological possibilities of his own time. The "field" thus became a way to rethink a model of production and perception adequate to the electronic age. It became one of Cunningham's preferred terms, denoting an idea of the stage organized by all-over width rather than perspectival depth—a landscape of dispersed attention rather than directed lines (i.e., diagonals pointing to centerstage). The word appears in the title of three Cunningham repertory works—*Field Dances* (1963), *Fielding Sixes* (1980), and *Field and Figures* (1989)—but the Events in particular were thought to produce "a 'field' situation rather than one in which the audience's attention is continually rationalized and directed to a hierarchy of activities on stage."[52]

51. Cunningham, in Arlene Croce, "An Interview with Merce Cunningham," *Ballet Review* vol.1, no.4, 1966, pp.4–5. In the same issue, Carolyn Brown published "McLuhan and the Dance," in which she applied ideas from McLuhan's *Understanding Media* (1964) to her work with Cunningham, drawing an analogy between the former's slogan "the medium is the message" and the latter's observation (in "The Impermanent Art," 1955) that "if the dancer dances, everything is there."

52. David Vaughan, "Cunningham: Continuity and Change," leaflet for New York Dance, published for the Theatre Development Fund by the NYDance Alliance, January 1976, n.p., in Merce Cunningham Dance Foundation Inc. Records, Additions, (S)*MGZMD 351, box 234, folder 5.

If technology extends the human perceptual apparatus and nervous system, as McLuhan argues, then nowhere was this better evidenced than in the then-relatively new experience of watching television.[53] Cunningham saw television as inherently fragmented, unlike theatre and film. Continually broken up by commercials, television takes for granted that we can watch two separate things at once, enabling a split attention or multitasking ("we see the end of a program while hearing what's next on the channel, then comes a news flash about a third to happen next

53. For McLuhan, artists played a key role as the prophets of new technology, serving as the "antennae of the race" (Ezra Pound) or an "early alarm system" that discovers social and psychic targets and thus prepares the us to cope with change. Marshall McLuhan, *Understanding Media: The Extensions of Man* (1964), NY: Gingko Press, 2011, introduction to the second edition, p.16.

week").[54] Like sport, television provided Cunningham with an everyday template for the organization of time by a predetermined length rather than by meter, tempo, and musical phrase—think of a thirty-minute television show or a ninety-minute football match.

54. Cunningham, Lecture draft for Douglas College, New Brunswick, 1965, pp.4–5. The idea of television as fragmentation stands in contrast to later theorists, such as Raymond Williams, for whom it is characterized by "flow." Williams, *Television. Technology and Cultural Form*. London: Fontana, 1974.

Cunningham's thoughts on television as a medium differed substantially from a younger generation of artists associated with Judson Dance Theater (1962–64). Art historian Carrie Lambert-Beatty argues that Yvonne Rainer's choreography, like that of her colleagues, existed in dialectical tension with the new "profusion of things to watch" on television.[55] Judson artists were not making work directly in response to television, she argues; rather, a mediated televisual regime of spectatorship shaped their work at a deeper level. This was manifest in their use of temporality and pedestrian movement, in their interrogation of liveness, and in the way the photographic became a "structuring paradox" of their work—from Cunningham company member Steve Paxton making dances based on sports photographs (*I would like to make a telephone call*, 1964) to Rainer's *Trio A* (1965) as a flowing continuum that deliberately avoids photogenic pauses and eye contact with the viewer.[56] Yet televisuality, both as a temporal structure and regime of perception, is always a point of resistance and negation in Lambert-Beatty's reading of Judson. Rainer, for example, disliked television's standardization and synchronization of leisure time, and regarded multi-channel spectatorship during the Vietnam War to be an increasingly politicized activity: choosing what to watch was also a question of choosing what *not* to watch.

55. Carrie Lambert-Beatty, *Being Watched: Yvonne Rainer and the 1960s*, Cambridge, MA: MIT Press, 2008, p.11.

Such a critical consciousness is entirely absent in Cunningham, who—like many visual artists in the early to mid-1960s—embraced television as an opportunity for new experiences, sensations, and social relations. Cunningham's notes and interviews show an interest in technology that is formal rather than political: television opens up possibilities for duration and continuity, and suggests a way to synthesize fragments rather than to critically splinter attention. Particularly striking is Cunningham's assumption that live

56. Lambert-Beatty, *Being Watched*, p.160.

television provides a model of *presence*, rather than of mediation or alienation. Today, after decades of media critique, this equation might seem counterintuitive, but in the 1960s, television was almost always broadcast live rather than prerecorded. This is why, in a lecture draft from March 1964, just three months before the first Event in Vienna, Cunningham could make the observation that

57. Merce Cunningham, Lecture Draft for Hartford, CT, 19 March 1964, in Merce Cunningham Dance Foundation Inc. Records, Additions, (S)*MGZMD 351, box 29, folder 2, pp.10-11.

> Television has made us look differently [...] The renaissance perspective arrangement has an archaic flavor. Television, when "live and real" allows everyone to be seen, at every moment, to his best advantage.[57]

Cunningham goes on to imagine a dance company performing flexible time and space sequences that could be presented on several channels during the same hour—so the spectator has "do-it-yourself continuity via the channel switch." This euphoric image of television as a surfeit of options provides a stark contrast to Rainer's fraught politicization of selection as a tightrope act between corporate advertising and national propaganda. For Cunningham, television offered a field of durational continuity but also freedom of choice; changing television channels could thus be seen as an assertion and expression of agency.

Cunningham explicitly notes that the shifts of attention required by the Events, which quickly move from one dance excerpt to the next, are "like the possibilities of television, where you jump from one channel to another, making your own continuity."[58] Today we might question this analogy. Channel surfing produces a paradoxical type of continuity: disruptive, fragmentary, and choppy rather than immersive. Focusing on different elements of a Cunningham dance is hardly equivalent to the drastic changes of tone afforded by switching channels on television. Furthermore, Events were challenging for audiences in part because there was not *enough* interruption and downtime. "The concentration demanded by more than an hour and a half of plotless dancing is very considerable," observed one reviewer in 1973, "After a time one dance movement begins to look dangerously like another a few moments back, and

58. Cunningham, cited in Jennifer Dunning, "Special 'Events' by Merce Cunningham", *New York Times*, 24 March 1978, p.C3. He continues: "Almost everyone thinks that in theatre there should be a beginning, middle and end, but that's not the way things work any longer."

eye and mind both demand a respite."[59] Yet Cunningham envisaged his audiences making their own optical edit of a performance by deploying "eyeshift" (a term from perceptual psychology) to choose which dancers and parts of the stage on which to focus. With eyeshift, editing takes place individually for each member of the audience, rather than being directed by the choreographer.

59. Clive Barnes, "Merce Cunningham and Four of his 'Events': The Program", *New York Times*, 25 March 1973, p.69.

As is often the case, what artists intend to be new and liberating for an audience is not always welcomed by those habituated to traditional modes of spectatorship. Cunningham seems to have been perplexed by audiences' inability to focus for ninety minutes, assuming that habits forged with television and cinema would transfer effortlessly back to theatrical performance:

> An "Event" has no intermission. But people sit through movies for an hour and a half with no intermission. Theater should reflect what is around us. People are accustomed to think that if there is a ballet, there should be intermissions. It's just a tradition. People don't do that in their lives or see things that way on TV. TV programs and commercials make up a kind of continuity.[60]

What Cunningham neglects to mention is that film and television deploy mechanisms of climax and suspense to hold the viewer's attention. Television commercials function like intermissions—allowing viewers to talk or leave the room and replenish their capacity for focused attention.[61] Although Cunningham uses the metaphor of choosing channels as a way to describe eyeshift, ninety minutes of an Event is much more demanding than the equivalent time in film and television, precisely because his choreography is modular, rearrangeable, and above all non-narrative.

60. Cunningham, cited in Anna Kisselgoff, "Merce Cunningham Likes a 'Risk' in His Career," *New York Times*, 1 March, 1974, p14. See also: "We may be used to ninety minutes because so many Hollywood movies have been about ninety minutes. We've come to accept ninety minutes as a norm." Cunningham cited in Jack Anderson, "Ever-Changing 'Events' by Merce Cunningham," *New York Times*, 17 September 1982, p.C17.

61. Intermittent attention was (and continues to be) understood as the dominant mode of spectatorship at home—even though channel surfing goes against the primary motivation of television programmers, which is to sustain attention (i.e., not to switch to a competing channel). See Rick Altman, "Television/Sound," in Tania Modleski (ed.), *Studies in Entertainment: Critical Approaches to Mass Culture*, University of Wisconsin Press, 1986, pp.39–54. Much later, in 1999, Cunningham still found channel hopping to be a generative point of reference, observing that *Biped* gave him "the feeling of switching channels on the TV... the action varies from slow formal sections to rapid broken-up sequences where it is difficult to see all the complexity." Cunningham, cited in the Merce Cunningham Trust dance capsule, https://www.mercecunningham.org/the-work/choreography/biped/

It is telling that duration emerges as an artistic strategy in tandem with the rise of television as a continual domestic presence. Warhol's first experiment in durational film, the five-hour-and-twenty-minute *Sleep*, 1963), owes as much to the continual presence of television as it does to Cage's twelve-hour durational performance of Erik Satie's *Vexations* a few weeks earlier.[62] It was not until the 1970s that theatre and performance became more interested in duration, most emblematically in the work of Robert Wilson. His twelve-hour performance *The Life and Times of Joseph Stalin* (1973) included a refreshment area adjacent to the auditorium. Such works invite what performance theorist Richard Schechner has called "selective inattention": viewers comes and go, pay attention or don't, select what parts of the performance to follow, or leave the space altogether. Tellingly, he argues that selective inattention is "trained by television, because the ubiquitous sets are always turned on but often not looked at."[63] Although Cunningham entertained the possibility of ambulatory spectatorship for Events, especially those in museums, it was with the possibility of different perspectives in mind, not the prospect of wandering off entirely to socialize. Nor would he have been content for audience members to stay in their seats and fall asleep, as Wilson and others anticipated.[64] Dancers were another consideration: fatigue could compromise form or even lead to injury. Before the ninety-minute frame had been established, Carolyn Brown recalls that Event #2 in Stockholm was "a daunting, nonstop, intermissionless two-and-a-half-hour marathon"—an ordeal for the dancers, and for the museum, who requested that Event #3 contain an intermission.[65] In this handling of duration and attention, then, we see Cunningham occupying a middle ground between experimental and classical, risk and convention: he was not willing to expand the limits of audience attention to include inattention, nor to push dancers to the point of possible incompetence or failure.

62. See Greg Uhlin, "TV, Time, and the Films of Andy Warhol," *Cinema Journal*, vol. 49, no. 3, Spring 2010, pp.1-23, and Branden Joseph, "The Play of Repetition: Andy Warhol's *Sleep*," *Grey Room*, vol. 19, spring 2005, pp.22-53.

63. Richard Schechner, *Performance Theory* (revised and expanded edition), NY: Routledge, 1988, ch. 6, "Selective Inattention," p.196.

64. Philip Glass once quoted Wilson saying of their four-and-a-half-hour opera *Einstein on the Beach* (1976), "Well, you know, if you fall asleep, when you wake up it'll still be going on." Cited in David Sillito, "Philip Glass: Have a sleep during Einstein on the Beach." BBC News, 4 May 2012, http://www.bbc.com/news/entertainment-arts-17958400.

65. Brown, *Chance and Circumstance*, p.407.

VideoDance

If the Events offered Cunningham a way to explore dispersed fields of attention, then his experiments with video from 1974 onwards, by contrast, exerted a more stringent channelling of focus. His interest in video stemmed from his experiences of being filmed for television in the 1960s, powerful memories of watching Fred Astaire films as a child, and a longstanding openness to new technologies. From 1974 onwards, Cunningham made over eleven films and videos, most of them in collaboration with Charles Atlas, who worked for the company between 1970 and 1983. Atlas was initially hired as assistant stage manager, and promoted to videographer-in-residence following his film documentation of *Walkaround Time* in 1973. With Atlas's input as videographer and editor, Cunningham began making dances choreographed specifically for the camera. His notes and lectures evidence how the two artists together set about learning how best to handle new technological equipment in order to develop a new genre, the VideoDance.[66]

Cunningham had agreed to broadcast performances of his work from 1958 onwards,

66. Cunningham, 'Notebook - Dance on Camera Lecture,' 30 April 1980, Merce Cunningham Dance Foundation Inc. Records, Additions, (S)*MGZMD 351, box 30, folder 1. After Atlas's departure, Cunningham made two VideoDances with Elliot Caplan: *Deli Commedia* (1985) and *Beach Birds for Camera* (1992). Atlas returned to make two final VideoDances with Cunningham, *Melange* (2000) and *Views on Camera* (2005).

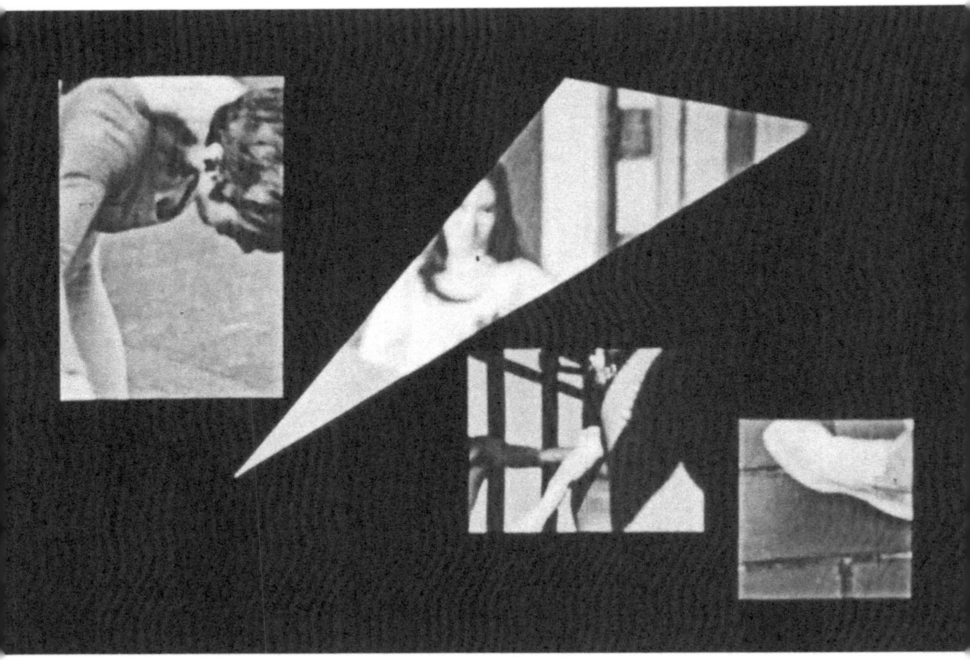

Fig.13

Stills from *Assemblage* (1968), also known as the *Ghirardelli Square Event*. Directed by Richard Moore. Broadcast on KQED, San Francisco. Note the geometric cut-outs and double exposures.

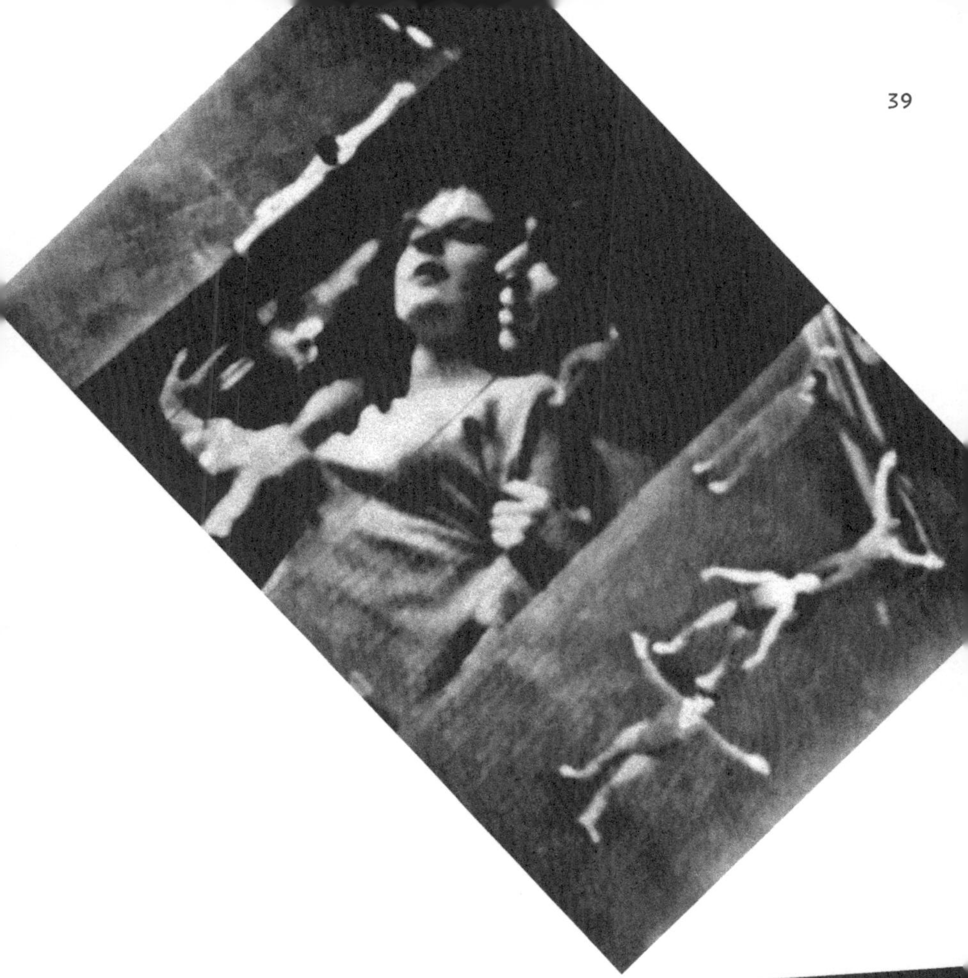

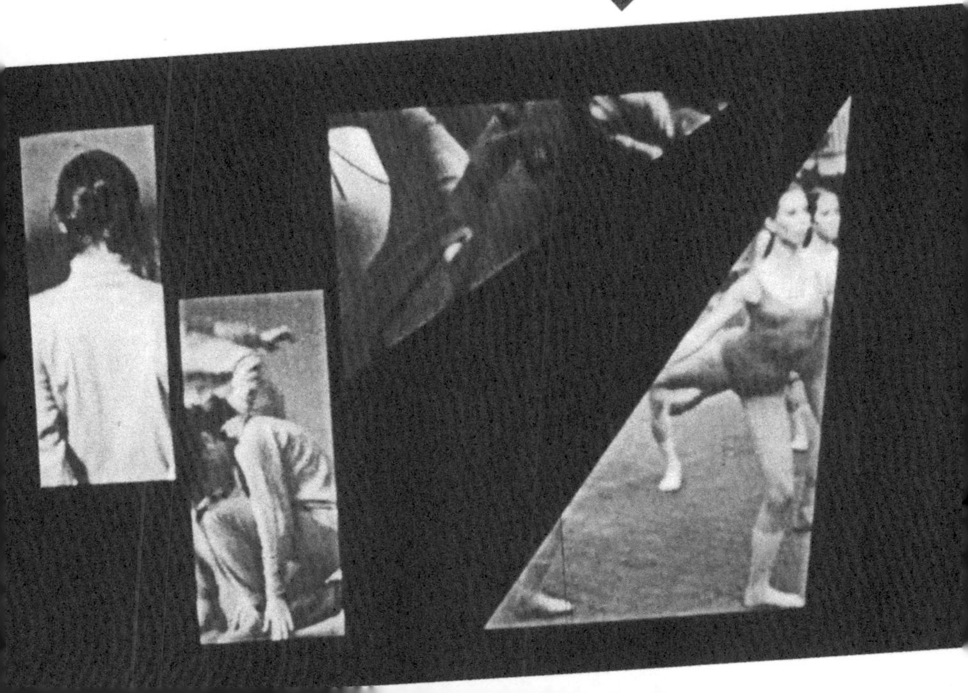

67. These include broadcasts for Belgian and German television in 1958, for Canadian television in 1961 (*Suite de danses*), for Swedish television in 1964 (*Night Wandering* and *Antic Meet*), a live production of *Story* for Finnish television in 1964, and for German television again in 1966 (*Variations V*).

primarily by European television companies.[67] This resulted in important documentation of certain repertory works, but was ultimately unsatisfying since each was characterized by a fixed camera that did little to replicate decentralized stage space and the experience of eyeshift. More successful was the one-hour film *Assemblage* (1968), also known as the *Ghirardelli Square Event*, directed by former Limon dancer Richard Moore and recorded outdoors in Ghirardelli Square, San Francisco, for KQED television, the local public broadcasting station. The outdoor location immediately disrupted any sense of fixed perspective, which Moore exaggerated by splitting the image into several simultaneous close-ups, presented as geometric cut-outs on a black ground, and creating sequences that double expose different perspectives. **[Fig.13]** The results are visually striking—dynamic and angular, almost Constructivist—but were not repeated in any of Cunningham's experiments with Atlas, in part, one suspects, because the choreography ends up losing its flow: the movements become fragmented and the dancers rendered decorative. *Camera Three: A Video Event* (1974), comprises two half-hour programs, recorded in New York City in 1973 and aired a year later on CBS, and is closer to what they would go on to produce. Cunningham's choreography is fused with experimental video techniques, quartering the screen into four boxes in order to disrupt a singular focal point of attention, while retaining a full view of each dancer's body.[68] **[Fig.14]**

These televisual mediations of Events pave the way for Cunningham's first VideoDances with Atlas. Television companies provided technical support to experiment with the moving image—equipment that was otherwise prohibitively expensive—but left Cunningham without directorial control. It would be several years before the company had the technical capacity to experiment with video in ways that more fully approximated multi-perspectival viewing.[69] Cunningham soon discovered that choreographing for video required a significant adjustment of his stage

68. *Camera Three: A Video Event* included excerpts of *Winterbranch*, *Second Hand*, *Sounddance*, *TV Rerun*, *Changing Steps*, *Landrover* and *Signals*, as well as footage of Cunningham's classes.

69. The live performance *TV Rerun*, in which Atlas and James Klosty appeared on stage with cameras during every performance, was the short-term, low-tech solution to Cunningham's interest in keeping the viewer's focus non-hierarchical and ever shifting.

approach in order for movement to be adequately visible on screen. As a result, the spectatorial freedom that characterized the "choosing channels" approach was now more prescriptively organized for the viewer. His first collaboration with Atlas, *Westbeth* (1974), has the grainy haze of early black-and-white videotape, but viewers can see the choreographer systematically working through questions specific to the new medium. The first section, which he dubbed the "Identification Sequence," shows all the dancers coming close to the camera so that they retain some individuality for the viewer.[70] **[Fig.15]** In the fifth ("Suite") section he marked up the floor with tape in order to keep all five dancers in full figure and on camera.

In subsequent VideoDances, Cunningham can be seen rethinking five aspects of stage performance: perspective, detail, speed, repetition, and editing. On a screen, perspective is constructed from wide to narrow (not narrow to wide, as in the theatre) and spatial depth is more extreme.[71] The area covered by the dance thus had to be reorganized as triangular rather than trapezoidal space. **[Fig.16]** Detail became more important: space had to be calculated to the inch (to keep the body in frame), while small gestures assumed more importance than onstage.[72] Speed functions differently: the eye can take in activity much faster on a small screen, since it holds the viewer's focus more intimately. Cunningham found that movement often looked too slow on video and needed to be accelerated; a position held for five counts on a stage, for example, only needed to be held for one on screen.[73] Repetition turned out to be a failure when recorded, rather than inexhaustibly fascinating, as when live. Repetition in order to get a good take was another hurdle: short takes, done over and over, were "one of the great energy killers" for the dancers.[74]

70. "The medium is an intimate one and if the person or persons remain too long in the back they lose identity." Cunningham, Notebook – Dance on Camera Lecture, 30 April 1980, n.p., Merce Cunningham Dance Foundation Inc. Records, Additions, (S)*MGZMD 351, box 30, folder 1.

71. "Space in film is deceiving. You can see a person's face in close-up and a few paces back from the camera you can see the person in full figure. A few paces further back and the person seems to have retreated a great distance." Cunningham, lecture notes "Dance with Camera," undated (probably 1984), p.12, Merce Cunningham Dance Foundation Inc. Records, Additions, (S)*MGZMD 351, box 30, folder 2.

72. "Every inch must be accounted for, or you overstep a mark marginally and lose an arm, a foot, half a face. It demands an accuracy about where you are." Cunningham, lecture notes "Dance with Camera," p.3.

73. Cunningham, lecture notes "Dance with Camera," p.5.

74. Cunningham, lecture notes "Dance with Camera," p.3. Cunningham notes that "after the fifth take of a sequence which has gone well for them, ill for the camera [...] they do it again with good spirits." "Well," said Cathy Kerr, "I've never given a seven-hour performance before." Cunningham, "Video/Film Dance Diary: 1981," p.6, Merce Cunningham Dance Foundation Inc. Records, Additions, (S)*MGZMD 351, box 30, folder 2.

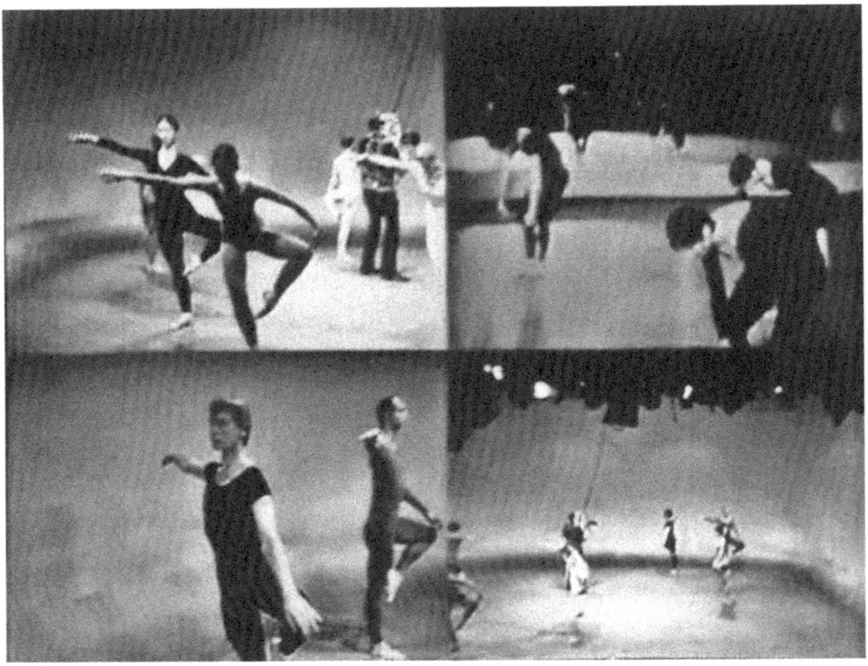

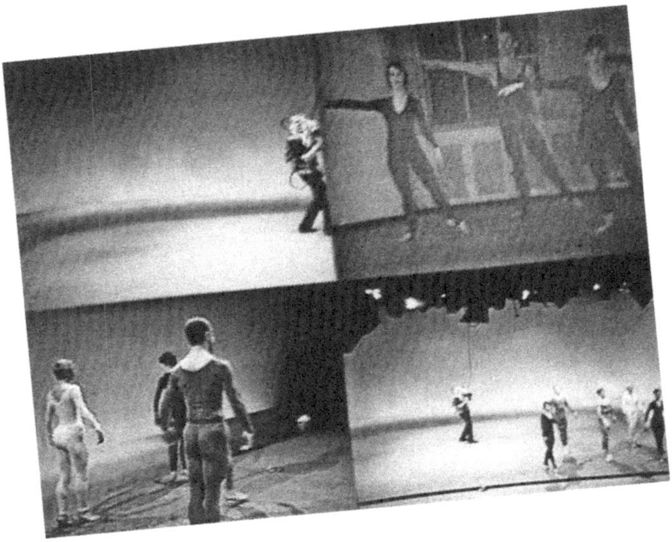

Fig.14 Stills from *Camera Three: A Video Event* (1974). Directed by Merril Brockway. Broadcast on CBS.

The left page shows a sequence from *TV Rerun* (1972); the right page shows *Changing Steps* (1973).

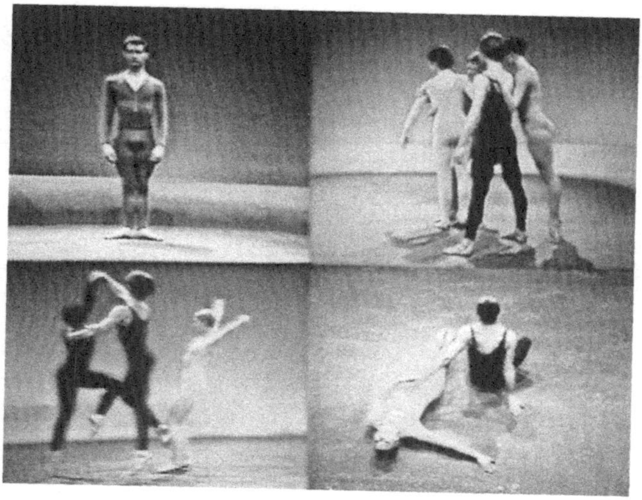

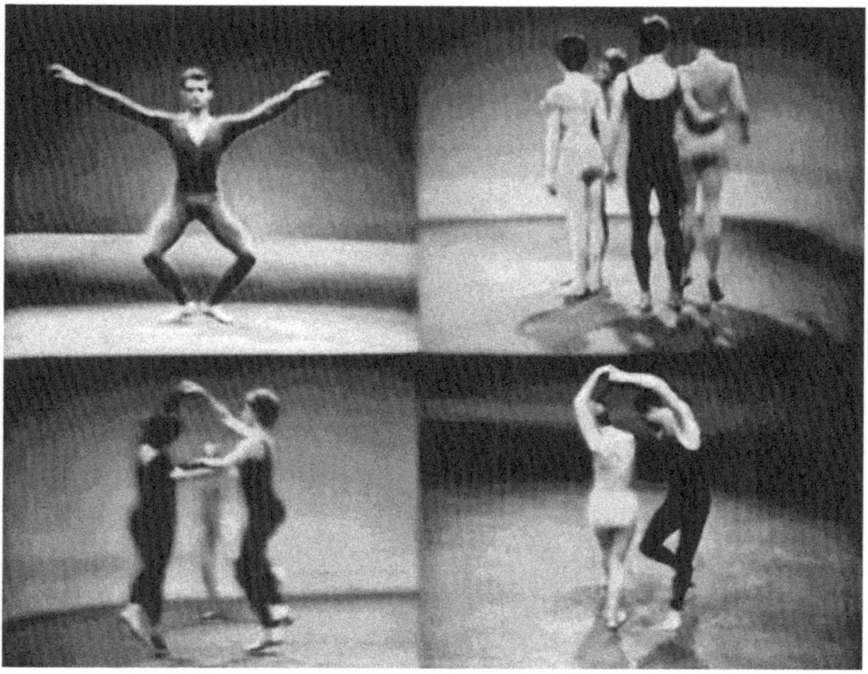

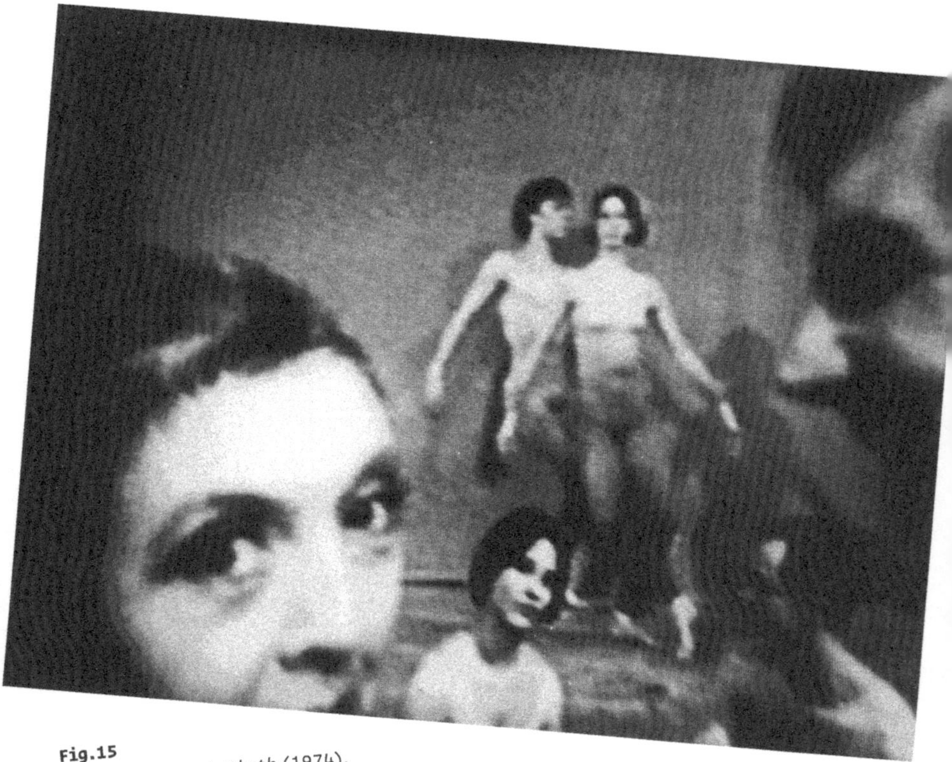

Fig.15
Stills from *Westbeth* (1974). Directed by Charles Atlas. The above image is from the section referred to as "Identifications," showing dancers in foreground, middle and background.

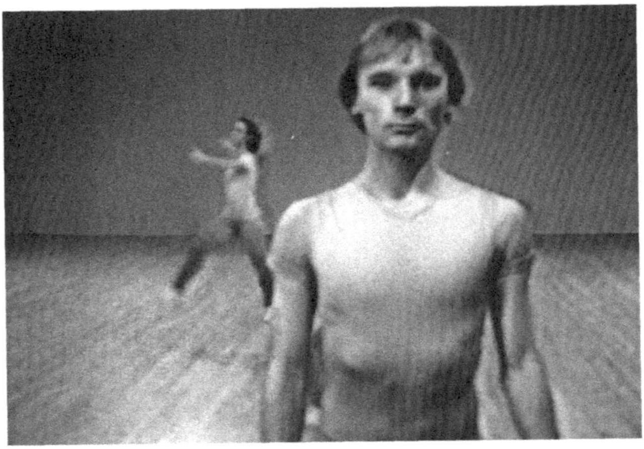

Fig.16
Still from *Fractions 1* (1978). Directed by Charles Atlas. On video, stage space appears triangular.

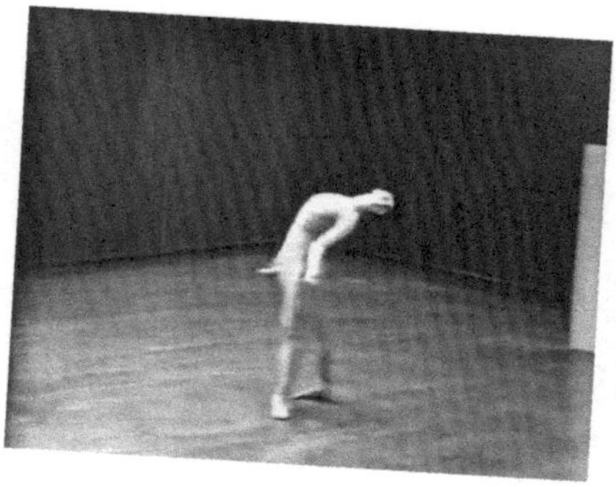

Finally, editing introduced additional complications because cuts produce a rhythm of their own that interfere with that of the dance. While most dance videos are edited on the beat of the accompanying music, Cunningham's work needed to be edited on the dance itself because the rhythms were unrelated to sound. The question of how to transition between footage of different spaces and locations without losing flow was a constant conundrum. Atlas and Cunningham's solutions included experimenting with three cameras—cutting between takes of the same sequence in order to capture momentum (e.g., the "video triangle" section of *Event for Television*, 1977). Another was the "travelling matte" effect, used at several moments in *Channels/Inserts* (1982), which enables a cut to last longer than one count.[75] **[Fig.17]** A third solution was a variant on the tracking shot, using dollies and cranes to keep the camera in motion: for one five-minute section of *Coast Zone* (1983), the camera and operator are pushed and pulled in a 540-degree circle around the perimeter of the space, while the five dancers continually shift their focus.[76] The mobility of the (portable) camera came to replace the mobility of the (seated) spectator's eye.

In working out these adaptations from stage to studio, the filmed choreography of Fred Astaire was a key reference point for Atlas and Cunningham.[77] Astaire was the first dancer to make the camera follow him, and not the other way round, and insisted that the dancer's body be seen fully from head to toe for the entirety of the dance

75. In film and photography, a matte is used to combine two or more image elements (usually foreground and background) into a single, final image. It involves silhouetting or masking off selected areas. In *Channels/Inserts*, the travelling matte sometimes looks like the first layer of dancing is being "cracked" across the screen, to reveal another layer of dancing underneath. At other times it looks more like an explosion of brushstrokes.

76. Cunningham, lecture notes "Dance with Camera," p.13.

77. Astaire has also been a key reference point for other artists including filmmaker Babette Mangolte (who filmed the work of Trisha Brown, Lucinda Childs, Cunningham and Rainer) and choreographer William Forsythe (e.g., the film installation *Antipodes I/II*, 2006).

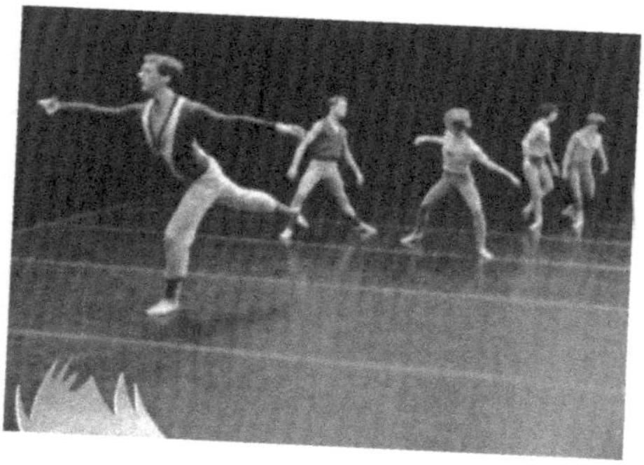

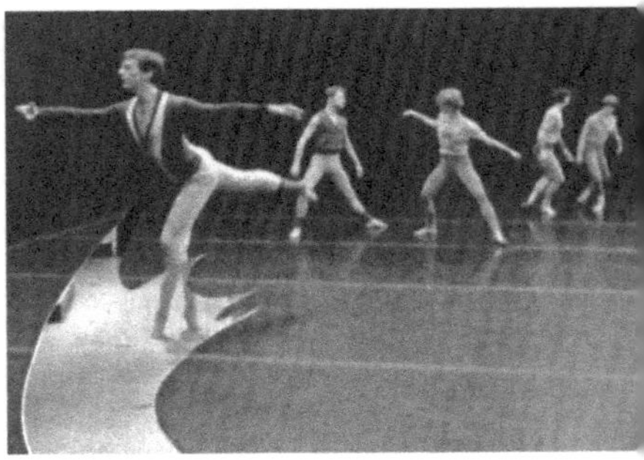

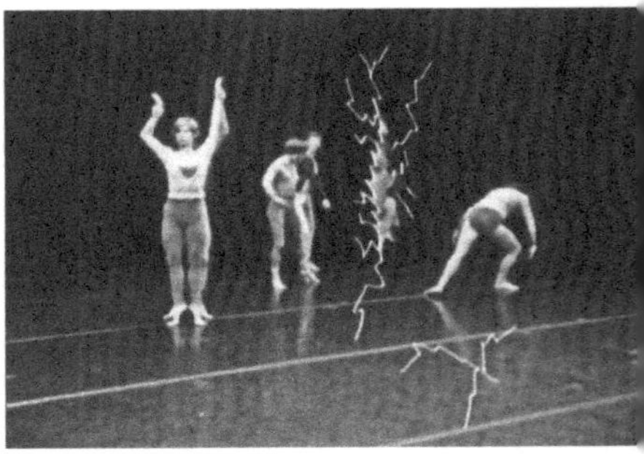

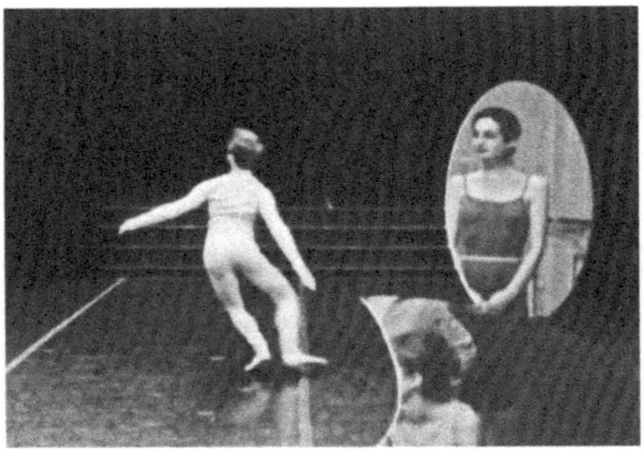

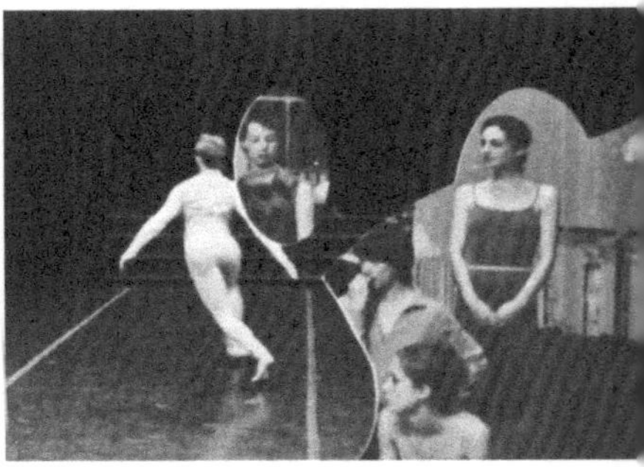

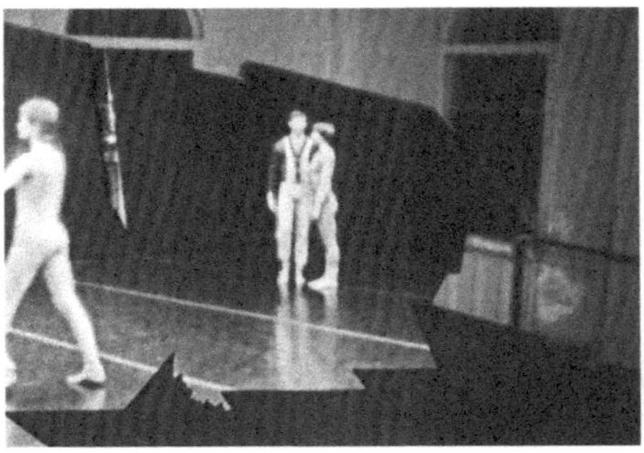

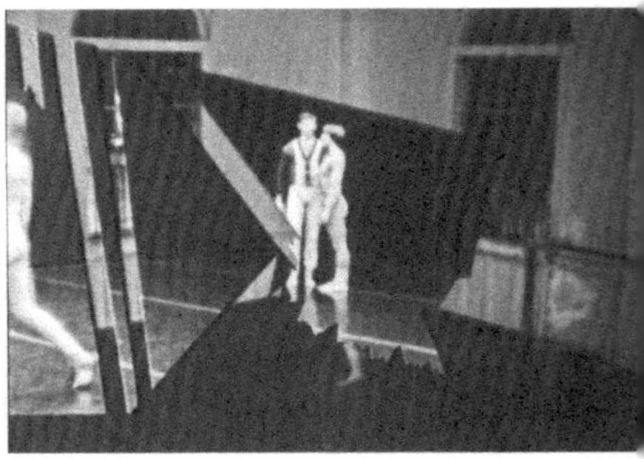

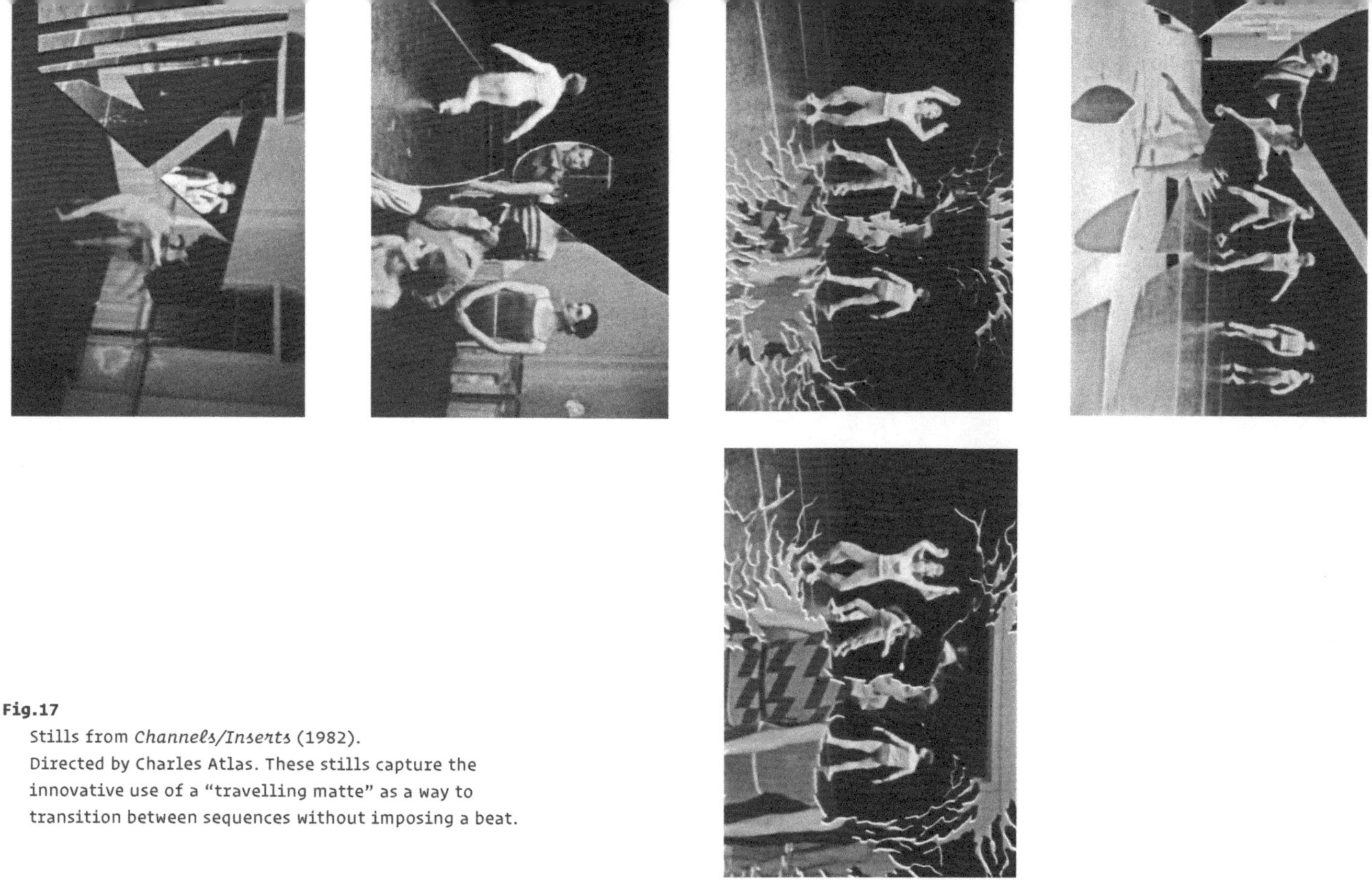

Fig.17

Stills from *Channels/Inserts* (1982).
Directed by Charles Atlas. These stills capture the innovative use of a “travelling matte” as a way to transition between sequences without imposing a beat.

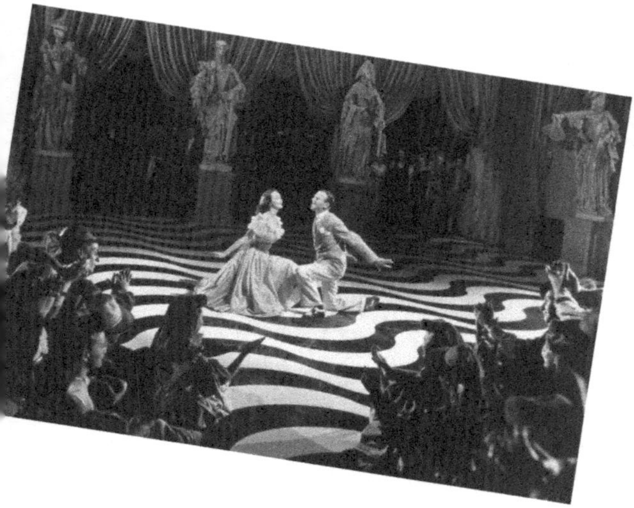

Fig.18
Fred Astaire dancing with Lucille Bremer in *Yolanda and the Thief* (1945). Cunningham described Eugene Loring's choreography in this movie as having "an extraordinary feeling of limitlessness in the space."

(rather than cutting between close-ups of the face, the body, and feet).[78] **[Fig.18]** Editorial cuts are infrequent and constitute only discreet shifts of perspective; the dancer remains more or less the same size within the frame, and there is never any distraction from the central performer(s). There is no emphasis on depth of perspective, only on the flow of movement continuity in space. Atlas and Cunningham, by contrast, sought to create a mode of recording more appropriate to non-narrative dance. They dispersed the viewer's focus across several dancers—and from multiple angles—in order to replicate a dehierarchization of stage space within the image.

78. The material in this paragraph is drawn from John Mueller, "The Filmed Dances of Fred Astaire," *Quarterly Review of Film and Video*, vol. 6, no.2, 1981, pp.135–54.

Atlas's two-screen edit of *Torse* (1977), for example, filmed with three 16mm cameras over the course of three days, deployed two mobile cameras (manned by Atlas and Cunningham) to capture close-ups, while a single stationary camera was set up for long shots. Atlas edited the results into a two-channel projection, which was screened in an exhibition context (rather than a cinema) due to its complicated dual interlocking 16mm projection system.[79] For the most part, watching this version of *Torse* is like simultaneously watching the stage from the auditorium *and* standing next to the dancer(s), as if each eye were located in a different part of the theatre. **[Fig.19]** At moments, the two screens synchronize into long shots (43'54, 54'00 and elsewhere) before

79. *Torse* was first screened at the New York Public Library for the Performing Arts, Lincoln Center, 3 April 1978.

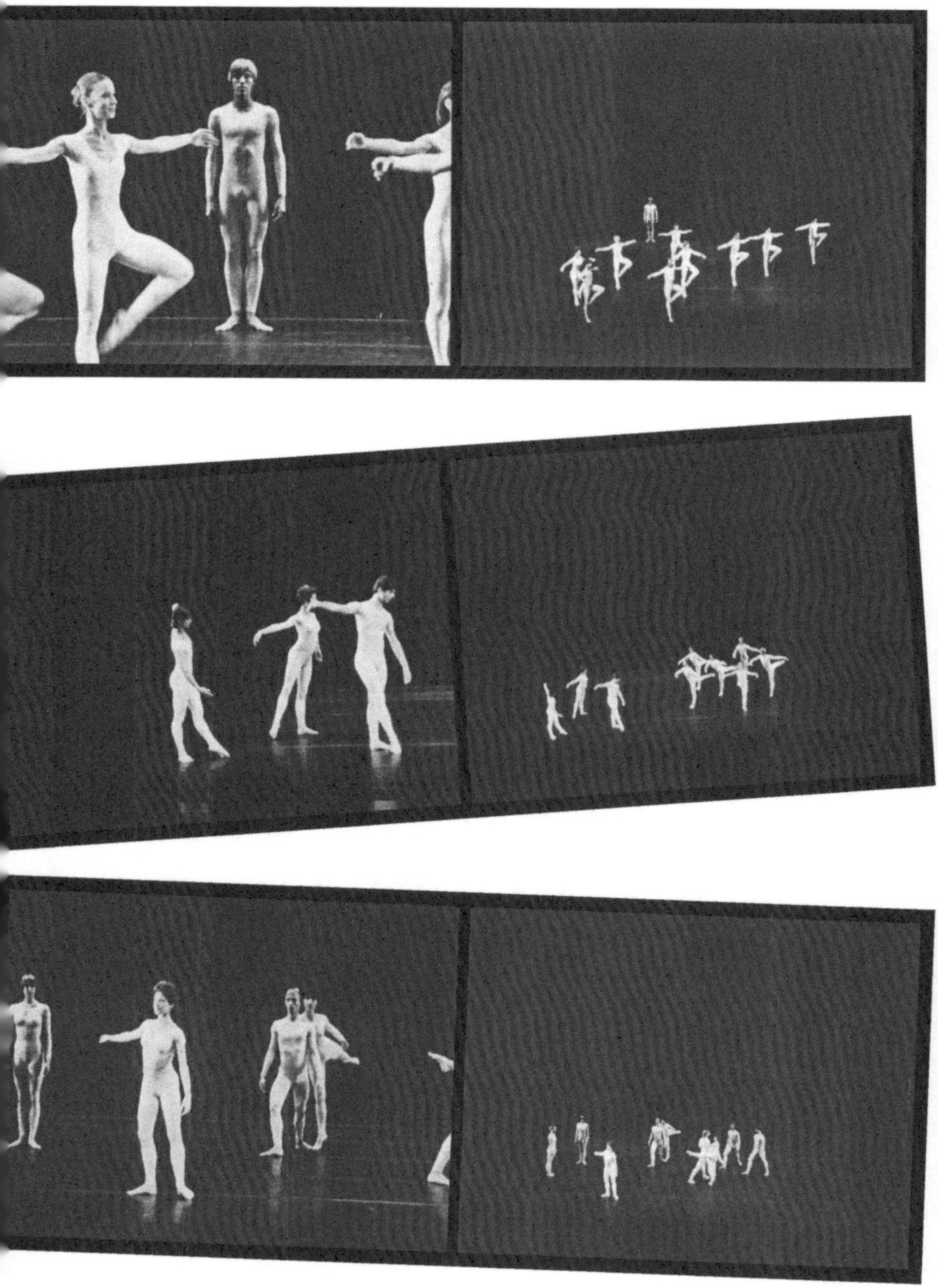

Fig.19
Stills from *Torse* (1978).
Directed by Charles Atlas.

 separating once more. This kind of experiment was costly and laborious, and could only be done with generous institutional support, in this case a residency at the University of Washington.

Back at Westbeth, Atlas returned to video the following year to tackle the same problem through internally regressing screens. *Fractions 1* (1978) begins conventionally, recording the dancers in the studio at Westbeth. Within two minutes, a pair of monitors become visible in the lower half of the frame, relaying different moments in the performance. In the last five minutes, these two monitors increase to four, only one or two of which ever correspond to the movements simultaneously taking place in the studio. The dancers performing adjacent to the monitors implicitly constitute a further "screen" or field of action. **[Fig.20]** As with *Torse*, Atlas's cutting speeds up towards the end of the dance, building momentum. During these sequences, the viewer's eyes dart about the screen, alternating between clear

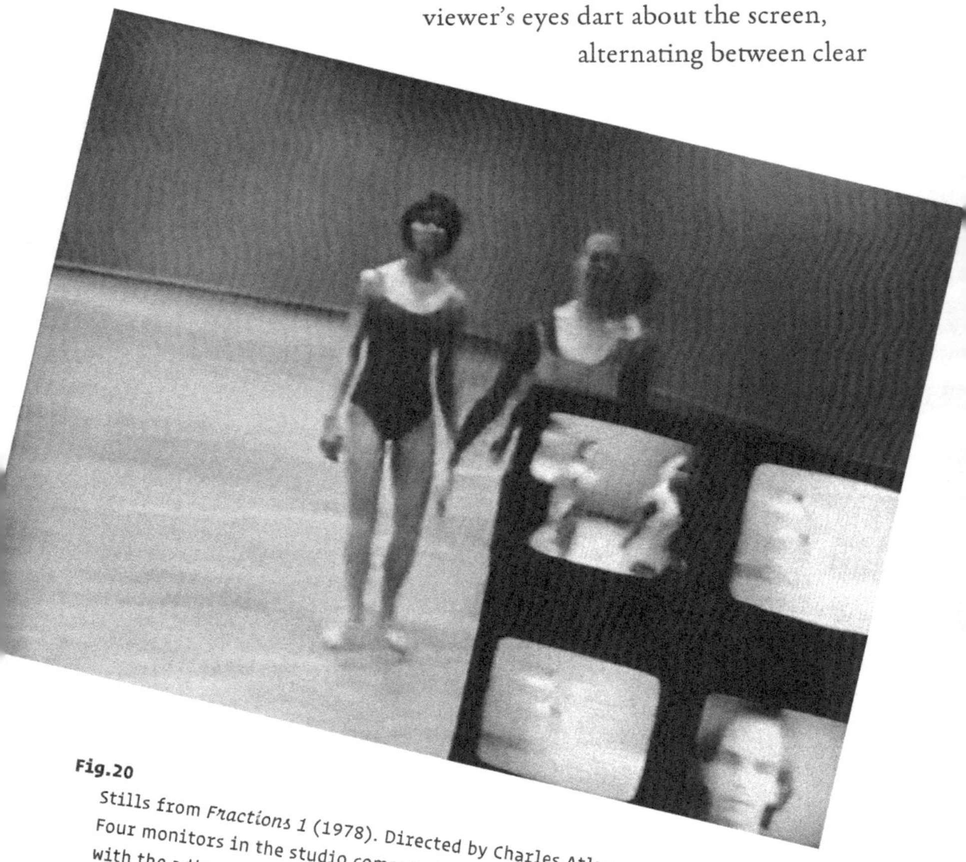

Fig.20
Stills from *Fractions 1* (1978). Directed by Charles Atlas. Four monitors in the studio compete for our attention with the adjacent dancers.

shots of the studio and the four monitors that occasionally impede this view. The perceptual freedom of the theatre, in which the viewer's eyeshift live edits the work, choosing which "channels" (dancers, sequences) to watch, is here reproduced within the internal composition of a single channel. At these moments, Westbeth becomes a transmedial space—less dance studio and more television studio, with each monitor showing multiple camera angles of the same sequence, sometimes including what appears to be offscreen or a "flashback" (as when Atlas suddenly switches to a duo in black and white from a group sequence in colour), creating a temporal relay between sections of the dance.

Cunningham's exploration of eyeshift in the Events was thus continued and compressed in VideoDance. For both formats, television was a formative point of departure. It provided a paradigm for dance as a flow of live, simultaneous activity, without plot or narrative, "edited" by the viewer in the manner of choosing channels. Rather than "polyattentiveness"—Cage's neologism for attending to several things at once—Cunningham was more interested in selective attention: the viewer's ability to choose what to focus on and when. Such a deregulation of vision, free from obligations to traditional hierarchy, connects his work to a longer history of modernist avant-gardists whose art dismantles automatized vision and makes perception lengthy and arduous—ironically, a world away from the commercial television that informed his understanding of duration and attention.

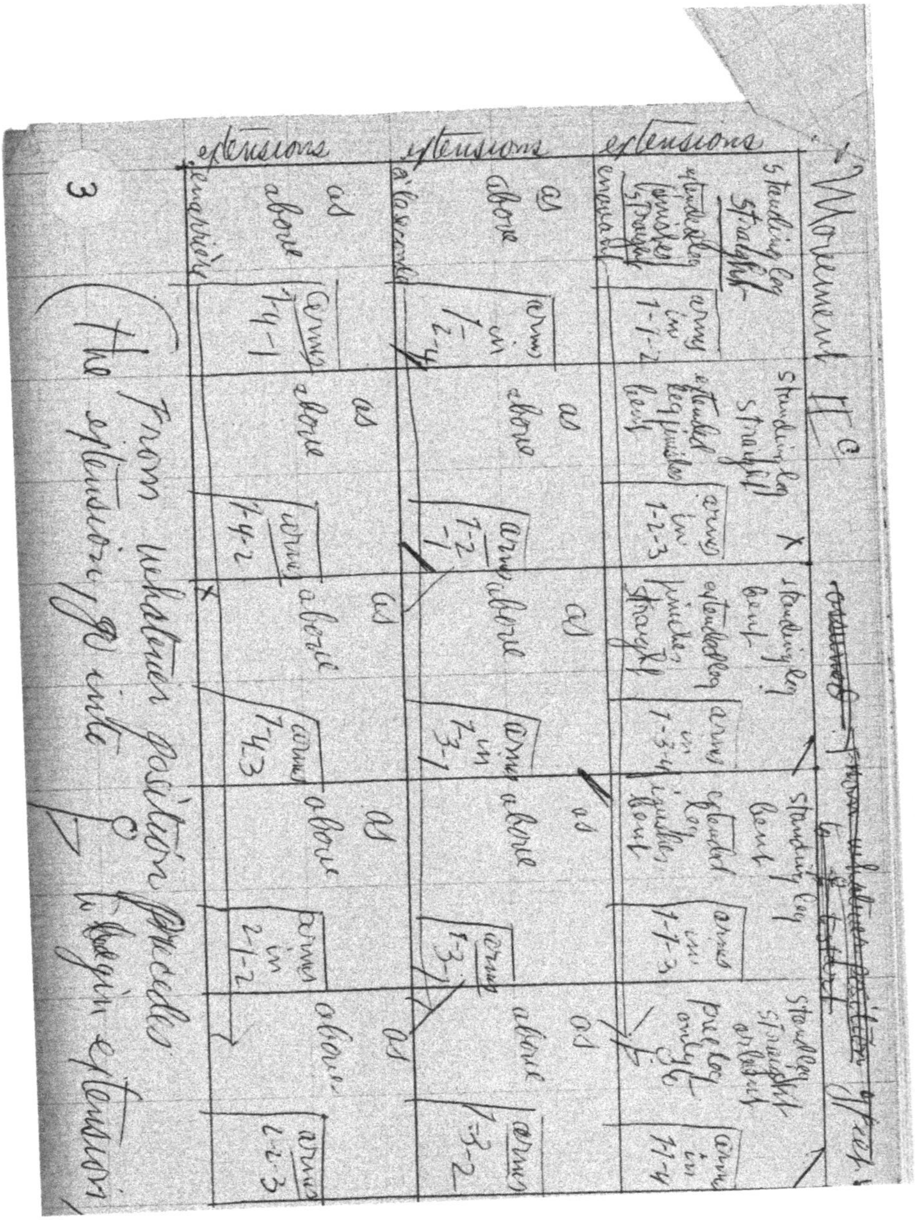

Fig.21
Score for *Suite by Chance* (1955). Reproduced in Merce Cunningham, *Changes: Notes on Choreography*, NY: Something Else Press, 1968, n.p.

Chance

80. "[Cunningham] would decide what the Event would be and the order often came about through chance—the sequence of what came." Chris Komar, oral history interview, 15 November 1993, p.76, Jerome Robbins Dance Division, NYPLPA. During my interviews with former dancers, several implied that Cunningham composed the Events by "rolling the dice" or using the I Ching.

81. Roger Copeland, "Merce Cunningham and the Aesthetic of Collage," *TDR*, vol. 46, no. 1, Spring 2002, p.18

One of the most frequent misconceptions about the Events, held even by some former company members, is that they were put together using chance techniques.[80] Copeland, for example, argues that to create the Events,

> [Cunningham] approaches his older works the way a film or video editor manipulates his daily rushes: cutting, assembling, and reassembling the fragments at will—although in Cunningham's case, it's not "will," but chance operations that often determine the new order of the fragments.[81]

From 1951 on, Cunningham frequently turned to chance when choreographing, in order to escape the tyranny of habitual preference. He tossed coins to determine the sequence of movements in *Sixteen Dances for Soloist and Company of Three* (1951), while *Suite by Chance* (1953) was choreographed using the I Ching, an ancient Chinese divination text from the ninth century BCE. Cunningham used cointhrows to enter a range of values on charts that would determine the "gamut" (Cage's term for a collection of sounds).[82] In *Suite by Chance*, this denoted a delimited range of movement options: isolated body parts and gestures (head, arms, torso, legs; bent, straight, tilted, etc.); duration (long, short, repeated); direction in space (whether the dancer faced the audience, the wings, or upstage). **[Fig.21]**

82. Cage developed the "gamut technique" in the *String Quartet in Four Parts* (1950). James Pritchett explains that "a gamut is simply a specific collection of musical materials to be used in a piece, defined before the rest of the composition continues [...] not simply a collection of pitches, themes, motives, or scales, but a collection of sounds of varying character and complexity." James Pritchett, *The Music of John Cage*, Cambridge, UK: Cambridge University Press, 1993, p.40. For a nuanced discussion of chance in *Suite by Chance*, see section four of Carrie Noland's "Coping and Choreography," *Digital Arts and Culture*, 2009, n.p., https://escholarship.org/uc/item/0gq729xq

While chance might have played a role in determining choreography for repertory works, Cunningham did not rely on it when assembling an Event. Not every piece could be included in the gamut. Certain dances were retired and never reappeared, such as *Story* (1963).[83] Other works existed initially as repertory but eventually found a more permanent home in Events, where they were performed in their entirety, such as *Crosscurrents* (1964) and *Signals*. Others were regularly excerpted: *Aeon*, *Scramble*, *Walkaround Time* (1968), the three movements of *Torse*, *Fielding Sixes*, *10s with Shoes* (1981), and *Roaratorio* (1983). Some works were made initially for film (such as *Locale*, 1979) and then found a life in Events; others were later abbreviated and reconfigured for Events, such as *Trails* (1982) and *Doubles* (1984). Some pieces never seem to have appeared in Events—e.g., *Summerspace* (1958), *Rainforest* (1968), *Biped* (1999)—while others existed only as Event material, such as *Exercise Piece no.1* (1978) and *Monk's Tale* (2004). Even if Cunningham had employed chance procedures to arrange the Events, the range of options had already been delimited.

The choice of excerpts further depended on which dancers in the company knew which parts. The majority of dances were made on specific individuals, and for the most part it was difficult to separate works from the dancers who performed them.[84] Cunningham was not just curating a (restricted) take on his back-catalogue to provide a satisfying evening of dance but selecting individuals that he liked to see perform. If Events in the late 1970s and 1980s were a vehicle for Cunningham's own performances—the structure supporting and framing his solo appearances—then this was less the case in the last two decades, when it was superceded by an interest in certain individuals.[85] Former dancers have implied that being included in an Event was one of the few ways they knew that they met the choreographer's approval.[86] Trevor Carlson, who worked in a range of capacities for the company

83. That said, the "Object" trio from *Story* was revived in 1985 for Events, and appears in an Event order titled *Paris Event #3*, dated 7/20/95.

84. When a dancer left the company, their parts would be inherited by the incoming replacement (Silas Riener, interview with the author, 22 March 2018). Dancer Patricia Lent recalls that Events were "a chance to perform repertory material that wasn't made on you; Event material was different because it belonged to others. After you'd been in the company five to six years, you were only performing work that had been made on you." Interview with the author, New York, 22 March 2018.

85. Cunningham stopped performing repertory in 1995, with a production of *Enter* (1992); his last performance in an Event, and with the company, was in 1999. Nancy Dalva, email to the author, 16 January 2019.

86. Greenberg again: "Merce never gave much evaluative commentary, so Events were where you could find out his approval or not, by what he gave you to do. But it was never about casting the individual first. It was the dance sequence first, then the individual." Interview with the author, New York, 8 March 2018.

from 1997 onwards, recalls that Cunningham would also give a dancer more prominence if he knew that their family was going to be in the audience. When preparing the Sculpture Garden Event in Minneapolis in 1998, Cunningham overheard that dancer Banu Ogan was a fan of Prince and was hoping he would attend the performance; that evening he gave Banu more solos.[87] In other words: selections were never just the material, but *the material in specific dancers' bodies*. The Event orders show personal interests interacting with (and contaminating) the objective procedures conventionally perceived to be the core of Cunningham's contribution to modern dance.

87. Interview with Trevor Carlson, via Skype, 22 February 2018.

The selection of excerpts was thus not organized by chance, nor was the sequencing. A close examination of the Event orders, worked out only a few days before or on the day of performance, reveals a recognizable structure over the five decades they were produced. In the late 1960s, this structure is still basic: excerpts of four or five works are presented in a straightforward sequence of self-contained units. Take, for example, the Gym Event at SUNY New Paltz in 1969, in which excerpts of *How to Pass, Kick, Fall and Run* (1965), *Field Dances*, *Canfield*, and *Scramble* (all 1967) were performed in unbroken blocks. **[Fig.22]** This compositional structure can be seen in other Event orders from the early 1970s, such as the ones for Ohio University and BAM in 1973. **[Fig.23]** But Cunningham had also begun to fragment his repertory works, as in the order for Event #80 at Westbeth (May 1973), in which five excerpts of *Changing Steps* are interspersed with four sections of *Canfield*, plus *Signals* and the finale of *Squaregame* (1976). **[Fig.24]** By the late 1970s, these excerpts are regularly punctuated by one or two Cunningham solos.

The structure is fully consolidated in the Event orders of the 1980s. **[Fig.25]** After a musical overture, the entire company (more or less) would be introduced via a large set piece (e.g., *Locale* 1 and 2, 1974, or the Jigs from *Roaratorio*). This would peel back to a duet or trio (e.g., the duet from *Exercise Piece*, 1975). After three or four excerpts there was a Cunningham solo such as *Loops*, *Hands*, *Fifty Looks*, or the *Chair Solo*. The following sections would offer clear contrasts in their energy, speed, and use of the stage: in an Event order for Lyon in 1982, for example, expansive sections (such as the diffuse first part of *10s with Shoes* were followed by close-cropped

Fig.22 Order for Event #9 ("Gym Event #5"), SUNY New Paltz, 27 February 1969. This is an unusual Event order: Cunningham lists the minutes in the left-hand margin, and there is an intermission. The running order is the opening section of *How to Pass, Fall, Kick and Run*, excerpts of *Field Dances* and *Canfield*, and the entirety of *Scramble*. Dancers' initials appear next to *Canfield*: Sandra Neels, Chase Robinson, Susana Hayman-Chaffey, Carolyn Brown, Mel Wong, Meg Harper, Jeff Slayton, Valda Setterfield, and Cunningham himself.

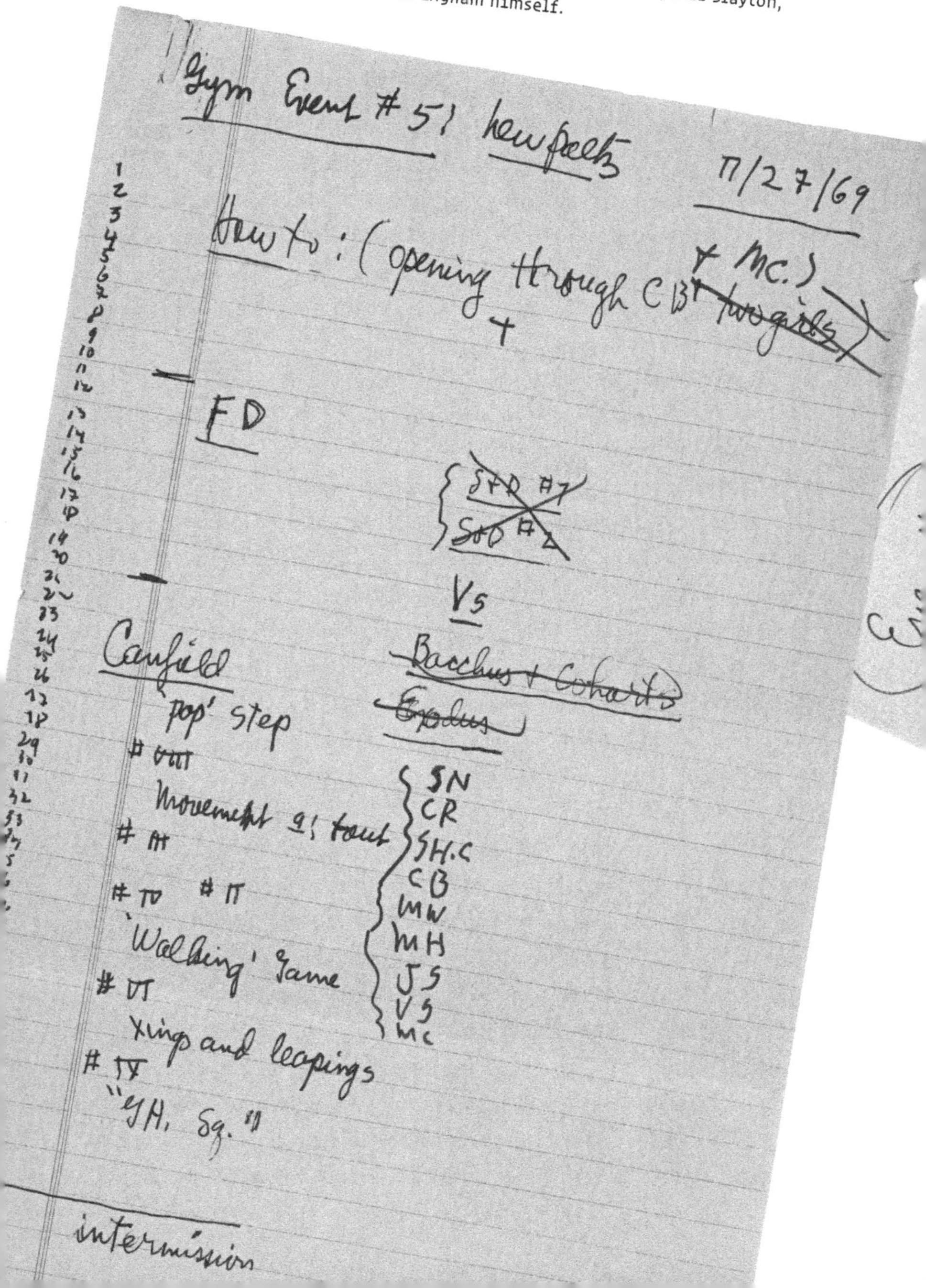

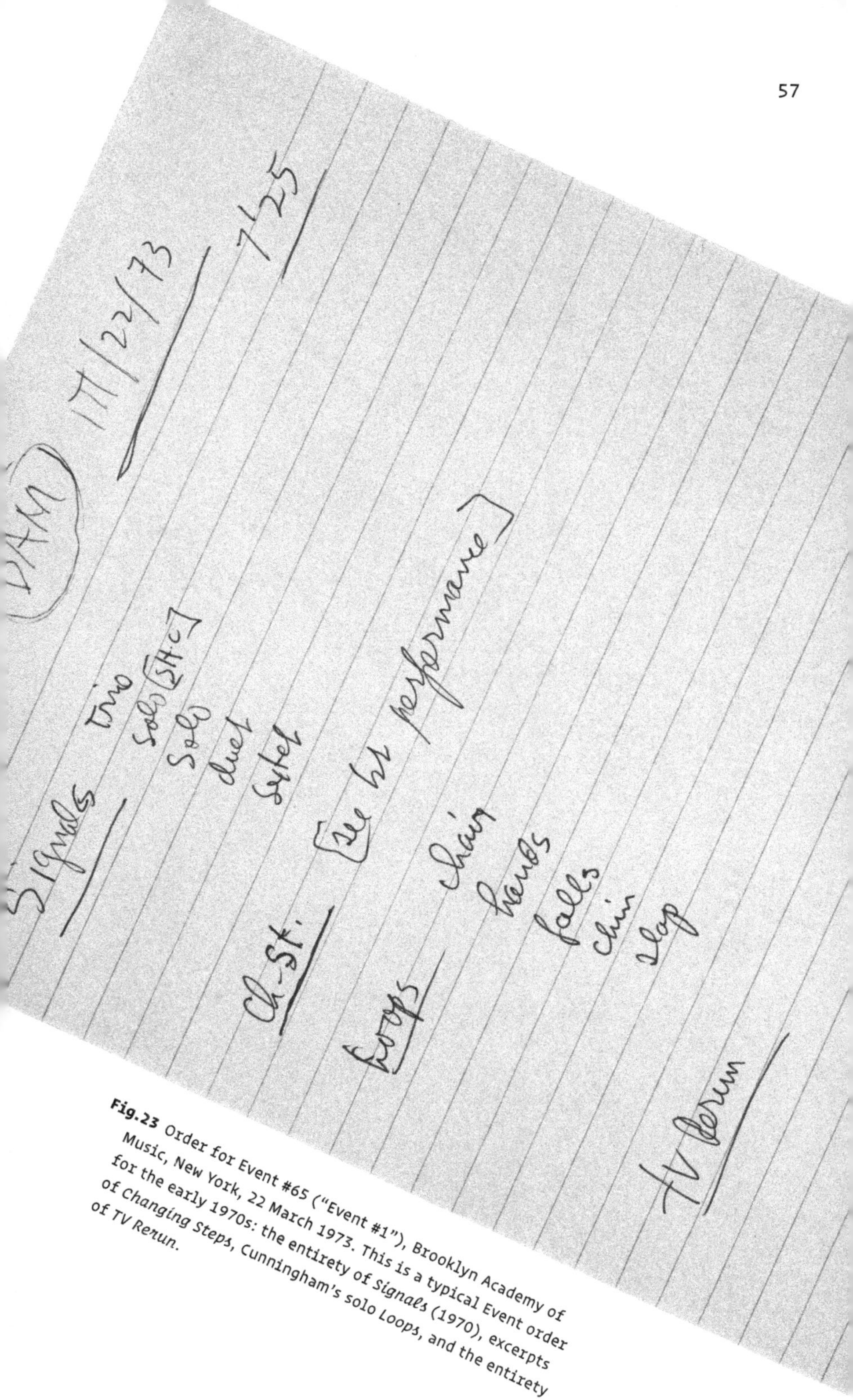

BAM 3/22/73 7:25

Signals trio
solos [SH-C]
solo
duet
sextet

Ch-St. [see 1st performance]
chair
hands
falls
chin
slap

Loops

TV Rerun

Fig.23 Order for Event #65 (“Event #1”), Brooklyn Academy of Music, New York, 22 March 1973. This is a typical Event order for the early 1970s: the entirety of *Signals* (1970), excerpts of *Changing Steps*, Cunningham’s solo *Loops*, and the entirety of *TV Rerun*.

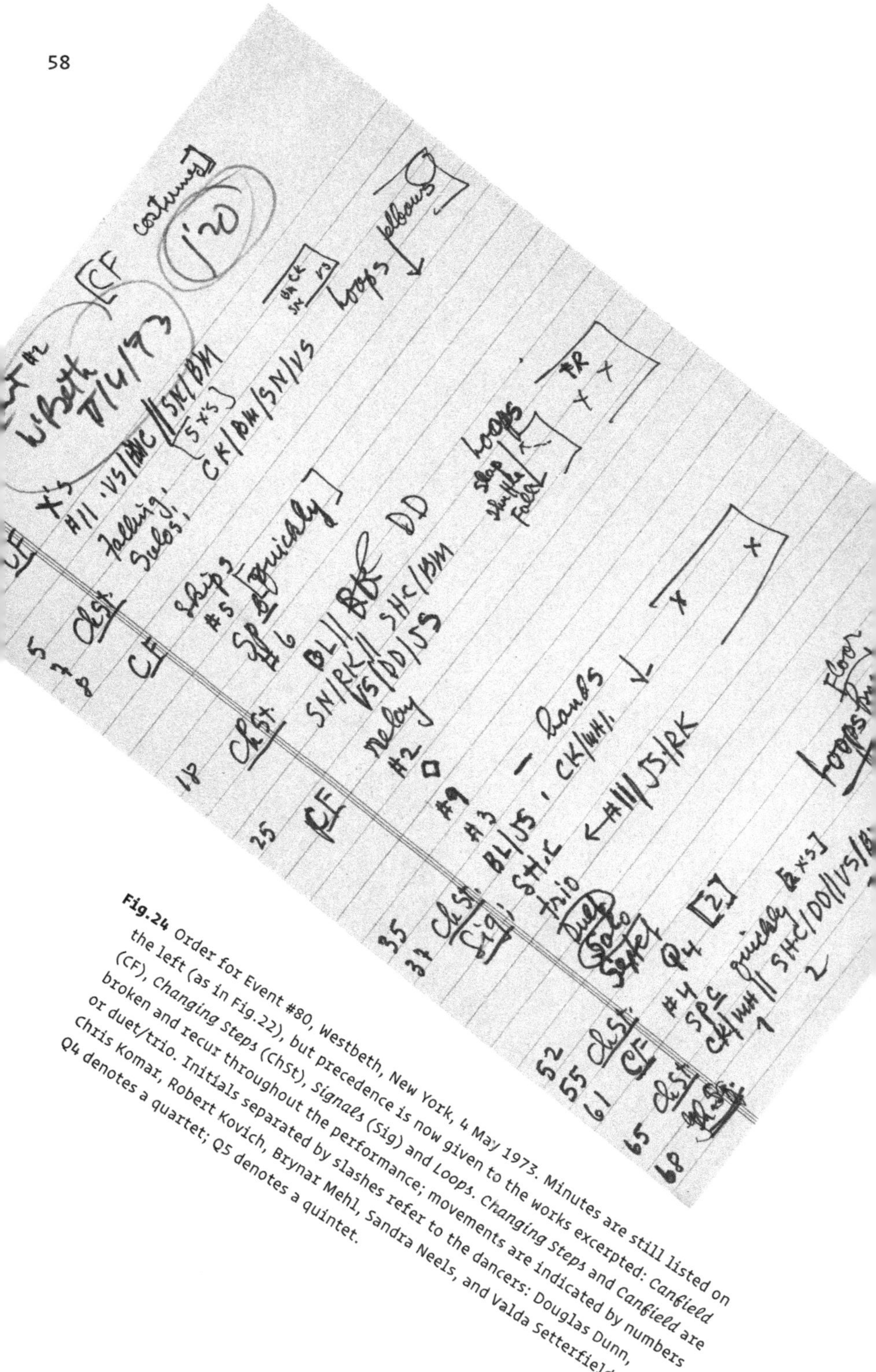

Fig.24 Order for Event #80, Westbeth, New York, 4 May 1973. Minutes are still listed on the left (as in Fig.22), but precedence is now given to the works excerpted: *Canfield* (CF), *Changing Steps* (ChSt), *Signals* (Sig) and *Loops*. *Changing Steps* and *Canfield* are broken and recur throughout the performance; movements are indicated by numbers or duet/trio. Initials separated by slashes refer to the dancers: Douglas Dunn, Chris Komar, Robert Kovich, Brynar Mehl, Sandra Neels, and Valda Setterfield. Q4 denotes a quartet; Q5 denotes a quintet.

Fig.25 Order for Event #317 ("Event #2 Lyon"), Auditorium Maurice Ravel, Lyon, 20 November 1982. This typifies Event Orders of the 1980s: no times are given, and certain works are dispersed through the performance (*Changing Steps*, *Scramble*, and the Jigs from *Roaratorio*).

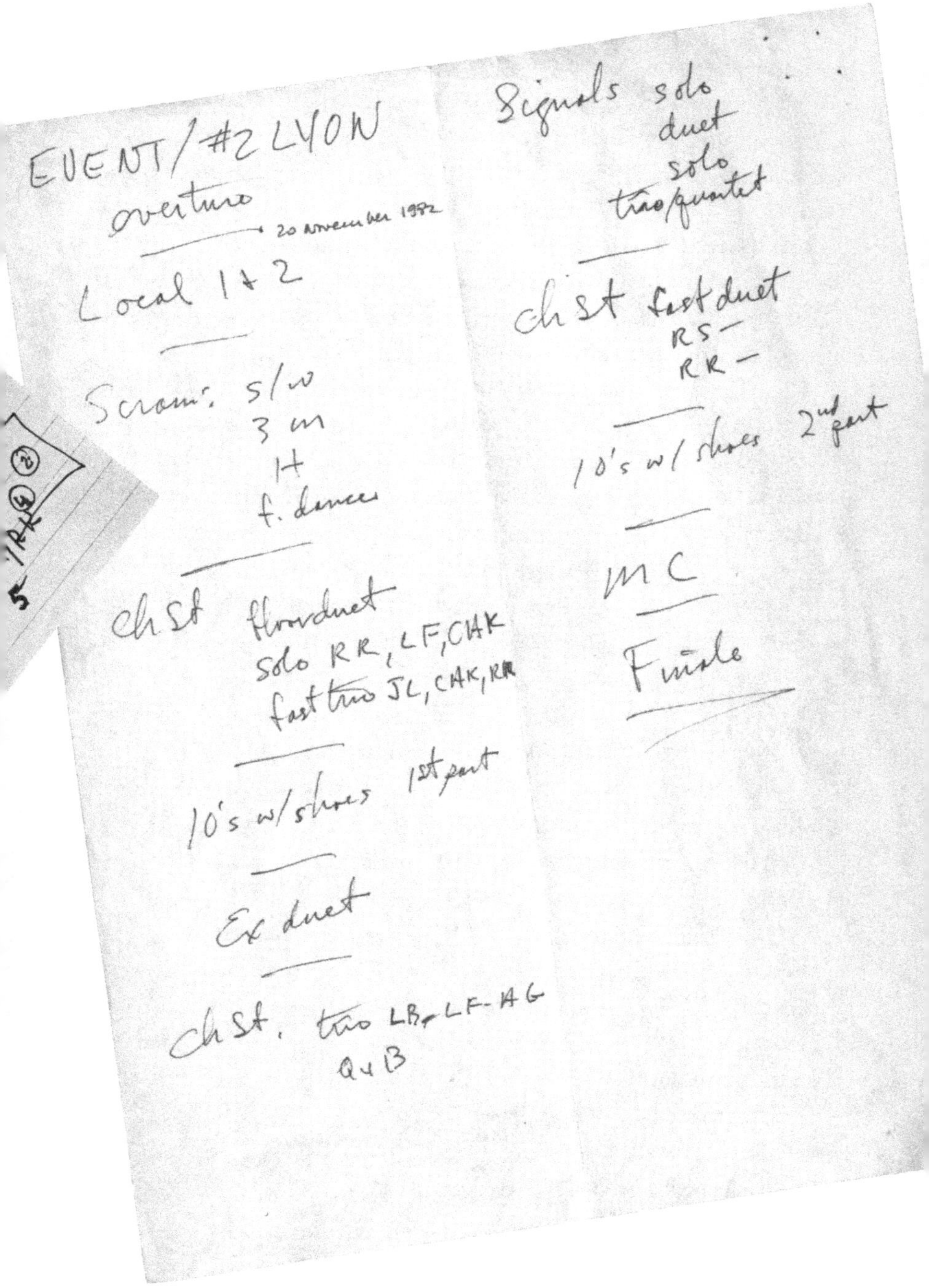

EVENT/#2 LYON
overture
20 November 1982

Local 1 + 2

Scram: s/w
3 m
H
f. dances

Ch St floorduet
solo RR, LF, CHK
fast trio JL, CAK, RR

10's w/shoes 1st part

Ex duet

Ch St. trio LB, LF-AG
Q + B

Signals solo
duet
solo
trio/quartet

Ch St fast duet
RS –
RR –

10's w/shoes 2nd part

MC

Finale

sections with a tight focus (*Exercise Piece* duet).[88] Two or three works would be broken up and reconfigured to recur across the whole program to create a pattern of relays and returns: *Changing Steps* broken into three parts; *Fielding Sixes* split into two; or any number of the eighteen sections from the modular and recombinable *Scramble*. Sometimes an entire work was performed as part of an Event (e.g., *Signals*); at other times just one movement was included (e.g., the trio from *Torse*, 1976). Eventually there would be another Cunningham solo, before a finale in which the entire company was brought back together on stage. The sections that usually filled this function tended to be existing repertory finales, such as the end of *Changing Steps*, *Points in Space*, or *Squaregame*, as seen at Grenoble in 1982, the Joyce in 1985, and Paris in 1995. **[Fig.26]**

88. I am grateful to Neil Greenberg for these observations, which emerged from our discussion of the order for Event #317 in Lyon, 20 November 1982, in which he performed. *Exercise Piece* was created for Events but later incorporated into *Points in Space* (1987).

This structure has very little to do with chance. In the words of Neil Greenberg, "You start with everyone, you end with everyone. Wide shot, tight shot. I teach choreography and the importance of unity, variety, and contrast, and that's the Events—very classical!"[89] Although Cunningham was radical in his use of chance procedures to free himself from habitual taste in his composition of early repertory pieces, the Event orders reveal the extent to which he remains conventional, even traditional, in his organization of theatrical experience. While the ninety minute duration is intended to push the limits of audience attention (as well as the dancer's ability to keep performing with precision), the Event orders nevertheless exhibit a familiar attachment to theatrical showmanship in their rhythm and pacing.

89. Neil Greenberg, interview with the author, New York, 8 March 2018. Another former company member, Silas Riener, notes how the Event orders mobilize the contrasting rhythms of each work: "fast big spatial things right up next to slow more stationary things." Email to the author, 13 July 2018.

As the company grew more successful in the early 1990s, fewer Events were performed, and touring new commissions was prioritized.[90] In 1995, Cunningham devised the MinEvent, a forty-five-minute version of Events that could be expediently added to an evening of repertory performances. The MinEvents are conspicuously denser in structure, packing more (and shorter) excerpts into the

90. Art Becofsky notes that after John Cage's death in 1992, "There was a vacuum. People filled it. Meanwhile, we were chunking along at an enormous pace still, of making work and touring. The bigger and better shows and the bigger and better stages with massive new works. It was all moving along and needed as much attention as ever, if not more attention than ever." Becofsky, oral history interview, 26 August 1997, p.143, Jerome Robbins Dance Division, NYPLPA.

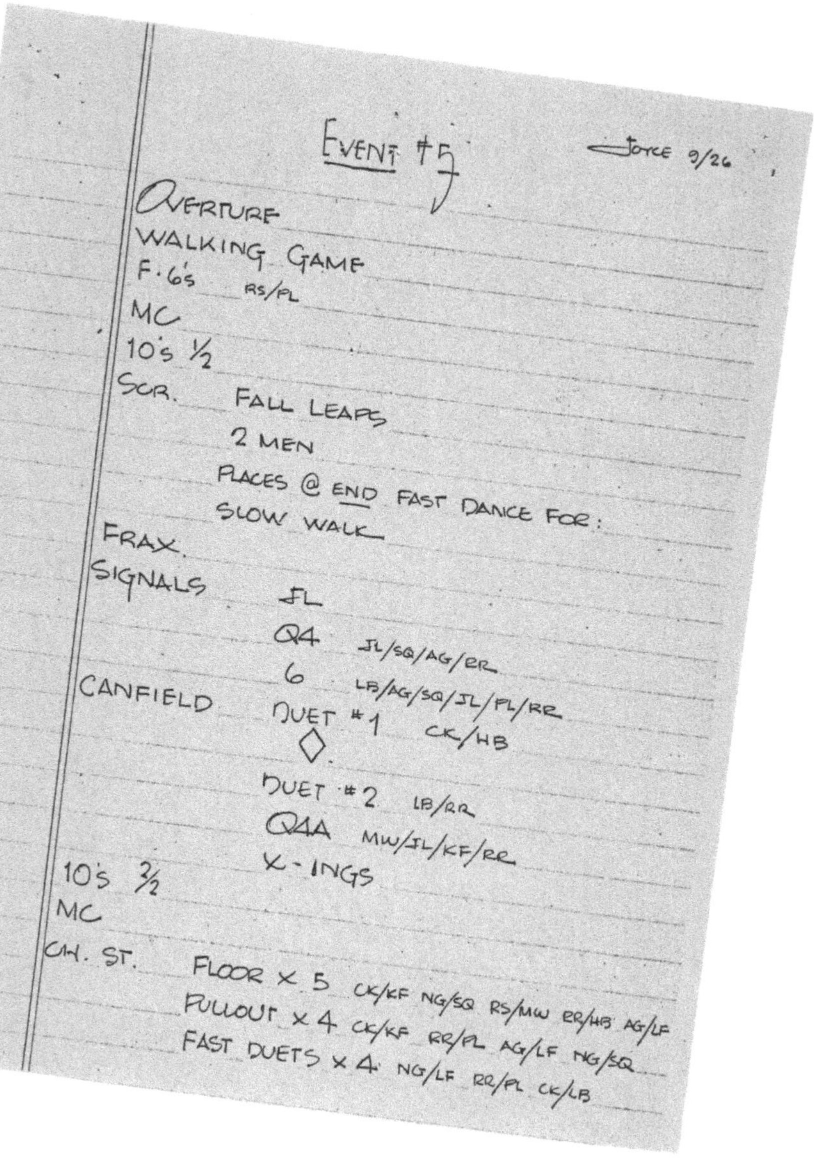

EVENT #5 — JOYCE 9/26

OVERTURE
WALKING GAME
F.6's RS/PL
MC
10's 1/2
SCR. FALL LEAPS
2 MEN
PLACES @ END FAST DANCE FOR:
SLOW WALK
FRAX.
SIGNALS JL
Q4 JL/SQ/AG/RR
6 LB/AG/SQ/JL/PL/RR
CANFIELD DUET #1 CK/HB
◇.
DUET #2 LB/RR
Q4A MW/JL/KF/RR
X-INGS
10's 2/2
MC
CH. ST. FLOOR × 5 CK/KF NG/SQ RS/MW RR/HB AG/LF
PULLOUT × 4 CK/KF RR/PL AG/LF NG/SQ
FAST DUETS × 4 NG/LF RR/PL CK/LB

Fig.26 Order for Event #365, the fifth of nine events at The Joyce, New York, 26 September 1984. A clear structure can be seen: an Overture, strategically positioned Cunningham solos (MC), and the Fast Duets from *Changing Steps* as a finale. Also included are excerpts of *Fielding Sixes* (F6s), *10s with Shoes* (10s), *Scramble* (Scr) and *Fractions* (Frax). This Event order is not written in Cunningham's hand.

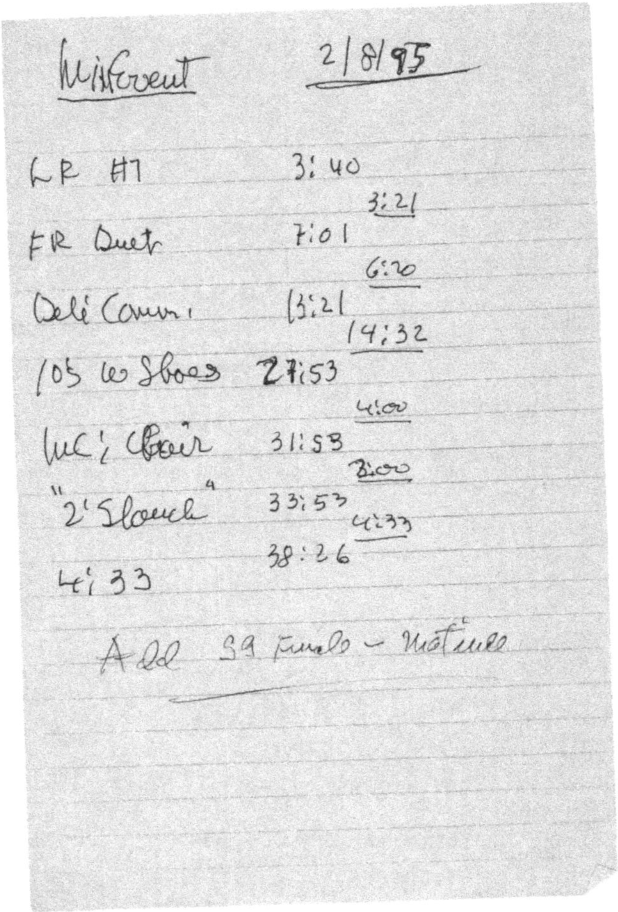

Fig.27 Order for a MinEvent dated 2 August 1995. Events were performed on 2, 3, 4 and 5 August 1995 at Palais Royal, Paris.

allocated time.[91] **[Fig.27]** The evolution of multi-stage Events from 2002 onwards further compressed and accelerated the performances, layering dances into three simultaneous stage areas. At Tate Modern in 2003, a ninety-minute Event was reconfigured as three simultaneous thirty-five-minute performances. Such multi-platform Events presented new mathematical challenges for Cunningham: how to organize the simultaneous unfolding of different excerpts on three stages, with dancers moving between them to perform seamlessly and on cue. The multi-stage Event orders show how mathematical calculations prevailed over the use of chance. The duration of each excerpt could only fluctuate by around fifteen to thirty seconds, requiring far more precision on the part of the dancers and limiting which sections could be included. **[Fig.28]**

91. Dancer Gus Solomons Jr. notes that the length of Cunningham's phrases in repertory works also decreased over the decades: "The attention span—the speed of the chunks—has decreased, consistent with our apprehension of the world since television. [...] the length of phrase has decreased. In other words, it comes in shorter shots, because we—the world—now perceive things in shorter chunks." Solomons, in Vaughan, "Cunningham and his Dancers: Conversation with Carolyn Brown, Douglas Dunn, Viola Farber, Steve Paxton, Marianne Preger-Simon, Valda Setterfeld, and Gus Solomons Jr.," in *Merce Cunningham: Common Time*, p.397.

Cunningham's attachment to precision and virtuosity helps to explain why he employed chance as a method of composition but never embraced *indeterminacy* in the resulting performance. Cage, by contrast, deployed both, relishing unforeseen outcomes—he once compared the performer of a score with indeterminate execution to "a traveler who must constantly catching trains the departures of which have not been announced but which are in the process of being announced."[92] Cunningham's only significant experiment with indeterminacy is the Judson-influenced *Story* (1963), a production with an eighteen-part structure whose order was determined by chance, but which the dancers could alter by giving movement cues to other dancers, resulting in a variable length of fifteen to forty minutes. The sets were made afresh each evening by Rauschenberg, while the costumes were chosen by the dancers from a large duffel bag onstage. After Rauschenberg left the company, *Story* was retired from repertory. Both the dancers and Cunningham seem to have found it stressful, albeit for different reasons. While

92. John Cage, "Indeterminacy," in *Silence: Lectures and Writings by John Cage*, Middletown, CT: Wesleyan University Press, 1961, p.39. This was nevertheless far from an anything goes free-for-all, and Cage clearly disliked certain interpretations of his scores. For a feminist discussion of Charlotte Moorman's interpretation of Cage's *26' 1.1499" for a String Player* (1955)—and the composer's view that she was "murdering" it—see Saisha Grayson, *Cellist, Catalyst, Collaboration: The Work of Charlotte Moorman*, PhD dissertation, CUNY Graduate Center, 2018.

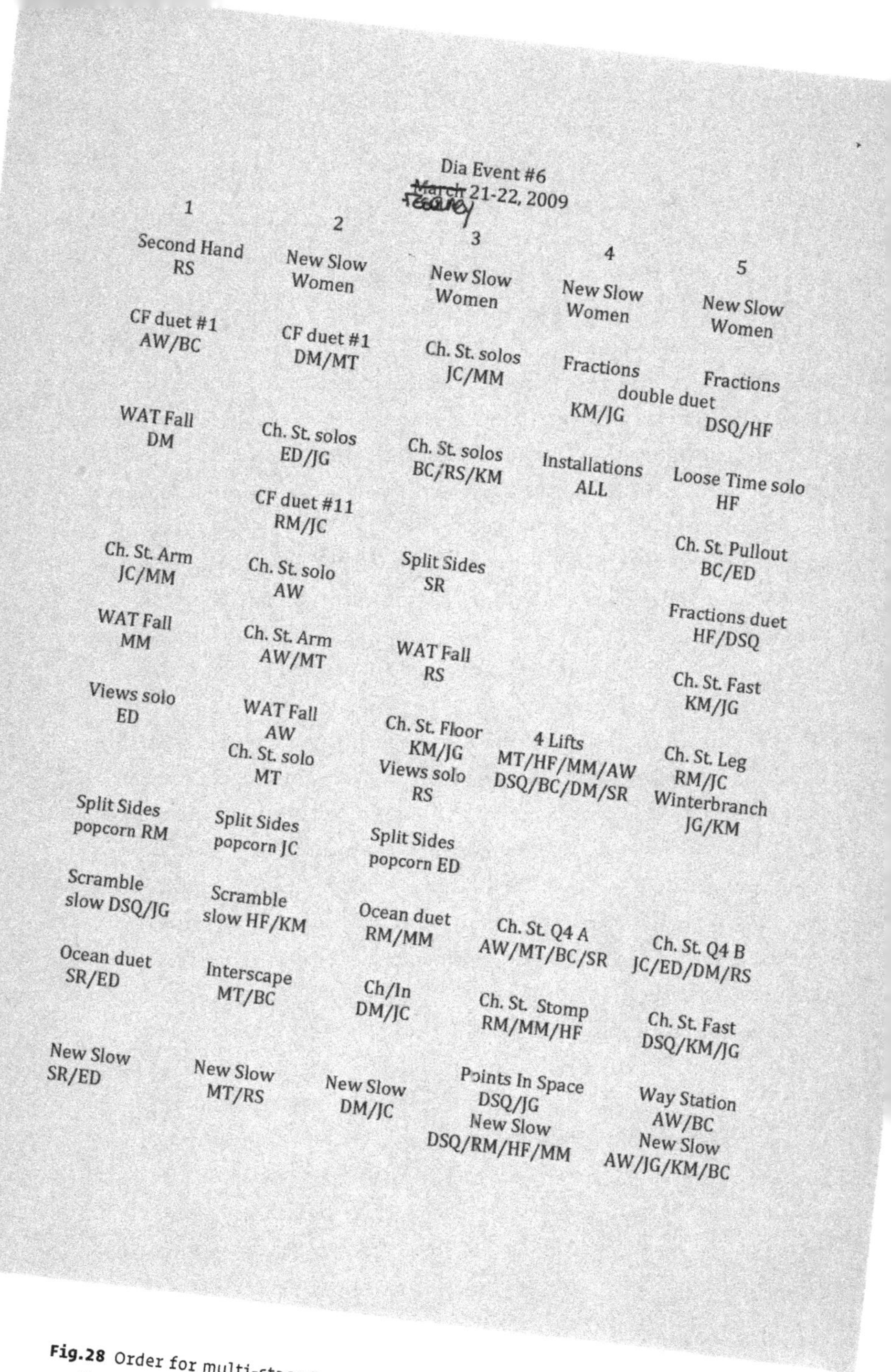

Dia Event #6
~~March~~ February 21-22, 2009

1	2	3	4	5
Second Hand RS	New Slow Women	New Slow Women	New Slow Women	New Slow Women
CF duet #1 AW/BC	CF duet #1 DM/MT	Ch. St. solos JC/MM	Fractions double duet KM/JG	Fractions double duet DSQ/HF
WAT Fall DM	Ch. St. solos ED/JG	Ch. St. solos BC/RS/KM	Installations ALL	Loose Time solo HF
	CF duet #11 RM/JC			Ch. St. Pullout BC/ED
Ch. St. Arm JC/MM	Ch. St. solo AW	Split Sides SR		Fractions duet HF/DSQ
WAT Fall MM	Ch. St. Arm AW/MT	WAT Fall RS		Ch. St. Fast KM/JG
Views solo ED	WAT Fall AW Ch. St. solo MT	Ch. St. Floor KM/JG Views solo RS	4 Lifts MT/HF/MM/AW DSQ/BC/DM/SR	Ch. St. Leg RM/JC Winterbranch JG/KM
Split Sides popcorn RM	Split Sides popcorn JC	Split Sides popcorn ED		
Scramble slow DSQ/JG	Scramble slow HF/KM	Ocean duet RM/MM	Ch. St. Q4 A AW/MT/BC/SR	Ch. St. Q4 B JC/ED/DM/RS
Ocean duet SR/ED	Interscape MT/BC	Ch/In DM/JC	Ch. St. Stomp RM/MM/HF	Ch. St. Fast DSQ/KM/JG
New Slow SR/ED	New Slow MT/RS	New Slow DM/JC	Points In Space DSQ/JG New Slow DSQ/RM/HF/MM	Way Station AW/BC New Slow AW/JG/KM/BC

Fig.28 Order for multi-stage Events #750 and 751 ("Beacon Event"), Dia Beacon, New York, 21–22 February 2009. Note the same order was performed for two days running. *Changing Steps* and *Scramble* continue to be Event staples. WAT refers to *Walkaround Time*.

the lead dancers in *Story* (Farber and Brown) had interesting material to perform, the other members of the company were restricted to "small, repetitive, pedestrian movement vocabulary that offered few technical or improvisatory challenges."[93] As a consequence, dancers wanted to push the small window of indeterminacy they had been given by Cunningham—as when Barbara Lloyd decided to wear *all* the clothes in the duffel bag, or when she chose to remove her clothes entirely. The choreographer was particularly unsatisfied when the dancers took liberties with pacing. *Story*, recalls Brown, "drove Merce to distraction when anyone exceeded or stretched the time beyond what he believed worked."[94] As dancer William Davis recalls, *Story* "was an unpleasant combination of ideas about freedom and still clinging to the hierarchy."[95]

93. Brown, *Chance and Circumstance*, p.439.

94. Brown, *Chance and Circumstance*, p.400. In Tokyo, Cunningham asked the dancers to do their *Story* phrases as slowly as possible, while he timed them. Paxton took excruciatingly long; Cunningham stopped watching him and walked off. Paxton kept going, dragging out his phrase to thirty minutes.

95. Davis, cited in Banes, "Materials for an article on *Story* by Merce Cunningham," Merce Cunningham Dance Foundation Inc. Records, Additions, (S)*MGZMD 351, box 28, folder 2.

After *Story*, indeterminacy was restricted, and resurfaced only in the most controlled set-ups—such as a brief sequence in *Signals* when the dancers line up in random order, and then dance a sequence associated with that position. The one exception to the rule, frequently (and joyously) recalled by dancers, took place at Berkeley in August 1971, when Cunningham realized that the company had committed to an extra date at the end of their residency but had nothing to perform. Cage suggested a variant on his *Musicircus* (1967), a scoreless, four-hour musical happening in which anyone who wanted to perform could do so, sharing the same time and space as everyone else (the poster wryly announced, "You won't hear a thing. You'll hear everything"). Cunningham allocated each of the eleven dancers (plus himself) a part of the stage in which to perform whatever they wanted, and for a set duration. Carolyn Brown recalls that "in the company's history, this was the one-and-only truly collaborative Event in which the dancers contributed ideas and choreography."[96] Cunningham seemed to enjoy the results, but the experiment was never repeated.

96. Brown, *Chance and Circumstance*, p.566.

Cunningham claimed that indeterminacy was impossible in dance because it wasn't safe to have dancers spontaneously moving around the stage, especially when tired and on tour. The subsequent development of Contact Improvisation by Paxton (and others) confirms that his objection had less to do with precaution than with a personal preference for precision and control.[97] After a peak of experimentation with spontaneously rearrangeable modules in the 1950s and 1960s, and a short-lived dabble with indeterminacy in *Story*, Cunningham returned to the security of fixed sequences by the mid-1970s. The multi-stage Events of the 2000s denoted the complete abandonment of chance and were the apogee of careful preparation and rehearsal.

97. Brown again: "I suspect he did not trust the dancers, and more importantly, giving up control of the structure, of time and space, was against his nature." Brown, *Chance and Circumstance*, p.441.

98. Cunningham, statement, May 1991, in Merce Cunningham Dance Foundation Inc. Records, Additions, (S)*MGZMD 351. See also Cunningham's interview with Philip Guerrard, September 1985, p.11, Merce Cunningham Dance Foundation Inc. Records, Additions, (S)*MGZMD 351, box 28, folder 3. Charles Atlas is unequivocal: "The idea of the Event was collage. Not cut-and-paste, that's later. Collage." Atlas, interview with the author, New York, 14 March 2018.

99. Kisselgoff, "Dance: "Event no.131"," *The New York Times*, 29 April 1975, p.39; Kisselgoff, "Cunningham's Followers," *The New York Times*, 5 April 1981. Ironically, Kisselgoff refers to the Events as most akin to collage when "the pieces did not stick." But sticking (*coller*) is the very definition of collage in visual art: gluing heterogeneous items onto a surface to create a play of figure and ground.

100. Roger Copeland, "Merce Cunningham and the Aesthetic of Collage," p.18. See also David Vaughan, "Cunningham: Continuity and Change," leaflet for New York Dance, published for the Theatre Development Fund by the New York Dance Alliance, January 1976, n.p. Merce Cunningham Dance Foundation Inc. Records, Additions, (S)*MGZMD 351, box 234, folder 5.

Collage

The Events are frequently described as collage, a conceit encouraged by the choreographer himself: "The Events are a collage, made up of elements from the repertory and new material developed especially for the particular Event."[98] The analogy has been repeated unquestioningly. "It is impossible to think of Mr. Cunningham's dances without the basic principle of collage," writes *New York Times* critic Anna Kisselgoff in 1975; he is "the Cubist of dance... [he] takes things apart, puts them together and believes firmly in the collage principle at work."[99] Copeland goes further, calling the Events "the single best example of collage in the entire history of the performing arts."[100] His claim rests on the Events' cut-and-paste structure, the use of a continually changing musical accompaniment unrelated to the choreography, and Cunningham's interest in width rather than depth on stage.

The Events, however, bear little relation to the visual art tradition of collage. The latter is predicated on the integration of heterogeneous objects and materials. To take two early examples,

Pablo Picasso's *Still Life with Chair Caning* (1912) includes oil cloth printed with a wood grain, and Kurt Schwitters's *Das Bäumerbild* (1920) includes newspaper, photographs, and bus tickets. **[Fig.29]** Rauschenberg's "combines" (1954 onwards) extend this principle into three dimensions, with items such as a quilt and pillow (*Bed*, 1955) and a taxidermied eagle (*Canyon*, 1959). **[Fig.30]**

Cunningham's Events, by contrast, draw on his *own* repertory material; to use a biological metaphor, they are endogamous and self-pollinating rather than exogamous and cross-fertilized.[101] Nor does he dismantle the movement sequences of individual sections, but maintains the integrity of each choreographic excerpt. Dances are never entirely mixed (e.g., a part of one work is never embedded within or alongside an excerpt of another); until the overlapping multi-stage Events of the final decade, excerpts were only of one dance at a time.[102] At most, the facings can change, as can the dancer's articulation. Costume, music, and lighting can also vary—so that in some cases, the choreography can convey a different atmosphere in an Event than in repertory performance.[103] But these various components do not render the Event any more akin to collage than any other theatrical production.

Cage's scores that invoke "mixing" at first seem to provide a more appropriate analogy for the Events. The score for *Williams Mix* (1952–53) documents the splicing and recombining of magnetic tapes in Cage's collection. The tapes include "city sounds," "country sounds," and "electronic sounds," among other noises from outside conventional musical composition, and are cut and spliced to form a work—of which the score is a document rather than a blueprint for repeat performances. By contrast, in *Fontana Mix* (1958) layered transparencies of abstract shapes can be placed on top of one another, to create an

101. Cunningham draws on movement vocabularies outside modern dance: genres that Carrie Noland refers to as "Higher Vaudeville," including Irish jigs and reels, Commedia dell'arte, tap, pageant, pantomime, and burlesque chase. Yet these are never inserted as wholesale appropriations into the composition (as is possible with performance) but filtered and modulated through Cunningham's sensibility, and often in the guise of rhythmic pattern. See Noland, *Merce Cunningham: After the Arbitrary*, p.153.

102. The exception is when Cunningham performed the solo *Loops* alongside the company performing *Changing Steps*. In the multi-stage events of 2003 onwards, excerpts of two or three works can be performed simultaneously but are not intended to be seen together as a collage—which would anyway be difficult in terms of perspective and focus.

103. The best-known examples of this are *Winterbranch* (1964) and *Quartet* (1982), which in repertory convey a sombre mood, largely due to the music and lighting, but as Event material seems more spirited. This is regularly noted by critics: see for example Robert Greskovic, "Event No. 145," *The SoHo Weekly News*, December 11, 1975, and Moira Hodgson, "Catching the Mind in Mid-Air," *Dance Magazine*, February 1976.

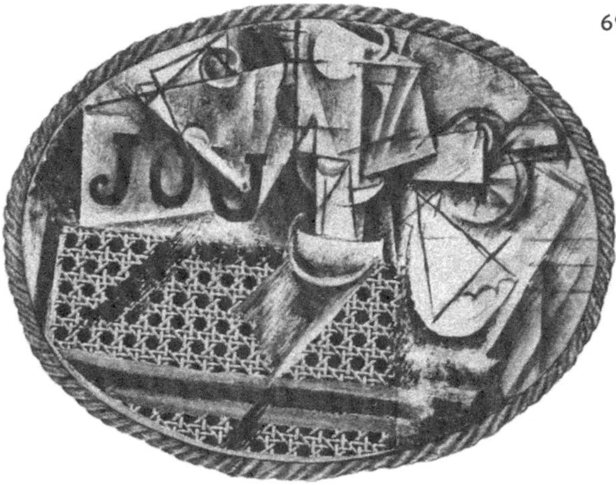

Fig.29
Pablo Picasso, *Still Life with Chair Caning* (1912).

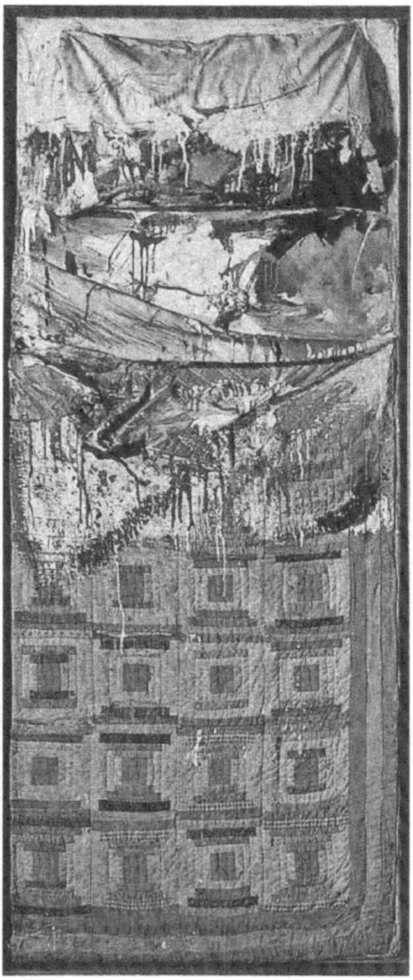

Fig.30
Robert Rauschenberg, *Bed* (1955).

indeterminate motor for composition *ex nihilo*, rather than a format for presenting a collection of sounds or one's own pre-existing work. The contemporary sense of "remixing," which began in the 1970s, is a different model entirely. It relies upon recording technology: individual tracks are removed or added, and the tempo altered, in order to produce a variation on the original song.

More than collage or mixing, then, Cunningham's Events are based on a closed system (his own work), which is further limited in its possibilities and permutations: sufficiently contrasting excerpts plus the availability of dancers who know the steps. Many channels are available, but the options are not infinite. Music historian Benjamin Piekut has compared Cunningham's creation of the Events to the performances of experimental music composers in the 1970s, many of whom accompanied the Events at Westbeth. Piekut shows that during this period, musicians gradually shifted from a dependence upon scoring and notation to electronic improvisation, in other words, to creation on site from a range of possibilities in the musician's repertoire. He argues that composers in the Cunningham circle, above all David Tudor, developed an "individual database of instrumental techniques, technical setups, stylistic and aesthetic tendencies, stand-alone compositions, and highly personal approaches to improvisation."[104] **[Fig.31]**

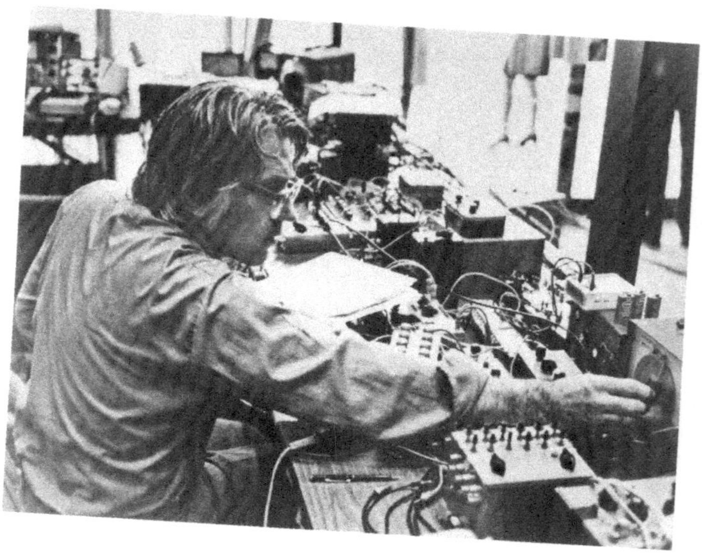

Fig.31
David Tudor and performance equipment, 1972.

104. Benjamin Piekut, "Not so much a program of music as the experience of music," in Meade and Rothfuss (eds.), *Merce Cunningham: Common Time*, pp. 115–28.

Piekut directly compares this model to the Events, quoting James Klosty's description of them as "a vast pooled resource from which single details and sections may be extracted out of context and reassembled into an unforeseen and novel unity."[105] Cunningham's own repertory could be thought of as a database or archive of possibilities that could be selected and combined in new sequences.[106] While less vivid than collage as an analogy, the database is a suggestive frame of reference for the Events since it anticipates a later moment of digital storage and search protocols—as well as Cunningham's use of LifeForms software to generate dance movement, from 1991 onwards.

The issue is not about finding the "right" analogy for Events. Collage, mixing, and the database all enrich our understanding of these performances in different ways. My point is that the kind of choreographic sampling and fragmentation Cunningham undertook in the Events was only possible because his work was, from the 1950s on, non-narrative and thus did not need to make sense as a story or lead up to a climax. In 1956, the four solos in *Galaxy* could be performed consecutively in any order, or simultaneously, or split into sections—and separately or overlapping. *Rune* comprises five parts running five minutes each whose order is variable and interchangeable from performance to performance, with no set beginning, middle, or end.[107] *Aeon* has sections that can be removed to make the work longer or shorter. *Field Dances* and *Story* (both 1963) are modular and can be performed in any sequence. These are just the works prior to 1964 that have a recombinatory structure. After the Event format was devised that year, a modular impulse continues to be found in repertory works until the early 1970s.[108] *Scramble* is basically structured like an Event, with eighteen interchangeable sections.[109] Certain performances of *Canfield* in the early 1970s are even listed as Events because the work had a variable structure and could last up to seventy-five minutes—yet each of these repertory

105. James Klosty (ed.), *Merce Cunningham*, NY: Saturday Review Press, 1975, p. 14.

106. Piekut describes the musicians as moving from "a repertory-work model to a database model." For Cunningham, the repertory *is* the database. There is no improvisation.

107. Even though, as Carolyn Brown notes, Cunningham eventually settled on one particular order for all performances of *Rune*. Brown, *Chance and Circumstance*, pp.251–52.

108. Works that can be performed in any order include *Scramble* (1967), *Canfield* (1969), *Signals* (1970), and *Changing Steps* (1973); there is also limited indeterminacy in the structure of *TV Rerun* (1972).

109. "*Scramble* is the iconic one. It's in so many Events because *it is an Event already*. It's the prototype. All the sections can be scrambled." Silas Riener, interview with the author, via Skype, 22 March 2018.

pieces claim a consistency of set, music, costumes, and lighting that is not true of Events.

One could argue, as Carrie Noland has done, that as soon as Cunningham began to compose by inventorying and numbering options, then permutation and recombination automatically ensue. This is because a list has no internal logic connecting one thing to the next.[110] A database is equally characterized by disconnected units that preclude narrativization.[111] This is, perhaps, part of what made the Events so difficult to consume in the early years—in Kisselgoff's words, "All 'events' thus follow the pattern of having no pattern."[112] Yet, as argued above, there *is* a logic underpinning the structure of Events. The orders are not just a list of one thing after another but arrangements intended to produce a satisfying aesthetic experience of contrasting rhythms, numbers of dancers, and occupation of stage space. Like so many aspects of Cunningham's work, the Events occupy a transitional middle ground: not the cause-and-effect of dramatic narrative, but neither the rote itemization of the postmodern list. They assert composition as *re*composition—recombining Cunningham's own output in ways that anticipate contemporary artistic strategies of aggregation and curation, both of which have developed in response to the surfeit of culture available through technological mediation.

110. Noland, *Merce Cunningham: After the Arbitrary*, p.45.

111. See Victoria Vesna, ed., *Database Aesthetics: Art in the Age of Information Overflow*, University of Minnesota Press, 2007, especially the essays by Lev Manovich and Bill Seaman.

112. Anna Kisselgoff, "Dance: 'Event no. 131,'" *New York Times*, 29 April 1975, p.39.

Collaboration

Consider this first observation, from Carolyn Brown, writing in 1975: "The truth is, Merce is no collaborator. He is a loner."[113] Now compare it to the following comment by video artist Charles Atlas, in 1997: "I learned collaboration from the master of collaboration, Merce Cunningham."[114] The discrepancy between these two testimonies, from two people who worked closely alongside the choreographer for decades, is revealing. Brown was noting the independence of the music and design that accompanied Cunningham's choreography: "He does not work *with* the lighting designer, set design, costume designer, or composer." Atlas, on the other hand, was describing how he and Cunningham worked closely to record and edit the videodances: "He was the best collaborator anyone could have."[115] Atlas's account is the dominant narrative to have come down to us: Cunningham is fêted as one of the greatest artist-collaborators of the twentieth century—in his endeavours with Cage and his circle of composers, as well as with visual artists who contributed sets, lighting, costumes, and other forms of support (like posters and prints for fundraising).[116] The Events, however, exponentially

113. Brown, in Klosty, *Merce Cunningham*, p.28.

114. Charles Atlas, in Matthew Yokobowsky, "The Real Charles Atlas: An Interview," *Performing Arts Journal*, vol. 19, no. 3, September 1997, p.26.

115. Charles Atlas, in Mary Lisa Burns, "Building a Body of Work: Charles Atlas and Merce Cunningham," *The Brooklyn Rail*, November 2010.

116. Three exhibitions have been specifically dedicated to Cunningham and his collaborators: "Invention: Merce Cunningham and Collaborators" at NYPLPA (2007) "The Collaborative Legacy of Merce Cunningham" at University of Arizona College of Architecture and Landscape Architecture (2011), and "Merce Cunningham: Common Time" at the Walker Arts Center and Museum of Contemporary Art Chicago (2017).

increase the number of Cunningham's collaborators. Events frequently featured a new composer for each venue—and multiple new composers, if the company was in residence for more than one night. In what sense did Cunningham collaborate with all these artists?

The colloquial way in which we understand collaboration—as a nonhierarchical meeting of minds engaged in ongoing exchange and ultimate co-authorship—does not describe Cunningham's approach, which was based on minimal dialogue and grew increasingly remote as the decades elapsed. Decisions about décor and music were outsourced to the artistic director and music director respectively, leaving Cunningham free to focus on the choreography. Asocial isolation, separation, and autonomy were the hallmarks of this collaborative method. For the most part, the commissioned artists and composers didn't even see the performance to which they had contributed until it was presented in public. More surprisingly, the dancers only experienced the sets, lighting and music for the first time at the premiere.[117]

117. Sometimes this was destabilizing, especially if the sound was particularly loud (dancers complained of feeling nauseous or off-balance), and it could be difficult to negotiate lighting by artists (e.g. Robert Morris's dark schema for *Canfield*, in which over half of the dance takes place in darkness). See Brown, *Chance and Circumstance*, p.381, and Brown in David Vaughan, "Cunningham and His Dancers," in *Merce Cunningham: Common Time*, p.403.

Perhaps with this in mind, art critic Calvin Tomkins has described Cunningham's approach as "blind" collaboration—suggesting not so much a chance encounter or exquisite corpse as happy accident.[118] Cunningham's method, however, was far from random or accidental. The decision to sever the relationship between music and choreography was a conscious reaction to precedents that subordinated music to dance or vice versa. In the ballet tradition, music was either commissioned after the dance was completed or existed prior to the choreography.[119] During the modern period, composers were usually commissioned to produce music that followed the rhythm and climaxes of the choreography. Henry Cowell, Lou Harrison, and Louis Horst

118. Calvin Tomkins, "On Collaboration" (1974), in Kostelanetz (ed.), *Merce Cunningham: Dancing in Space and Time*, Chicago: a cappella books, 1992, p.45

119. Marius Petipa created his dances and stage action before the music was written, and then gave Tchaikovsky detailed scenarios with instructions about character, tempo, and rhythmic structure: "the choreographer's creative vision took unquestioned priority over the ideas of his collaborators, particularly those of the composer." Matthew Naughtin, *Ballet Music: A Handbook*, Lanham, MD: Rowman and Littlefield, 2004, p.88.

(Martha Graham's resident composer from 1926 to 1948) all composed accompanying music by watching the choreography.[120]

120. Harrison hated the stigma of being a "dance-composer," while Cage detested being a dance accompanist and described it as "drudgery." Harrison, letter to Henry Cowell, circa 1940. Cage, letter to Lou Harrison, April 1939. Both cited in Leta Miller, "Henry Cowell and Modern Dance: The Genesis of Elastic Form," *American Music*, vol.20, no.1, Spring 2002, p.1.

In response, Cage and Cunningham sought a more egalitarian and independent way of working in which neither discipline was dominant. Their first collaboration took place in New York in 1944, using what Cage called "rhythmic structure" to create ageed-upon macro and micro divisions of time. Music and dance would be composed independently but came together at certain structural points. Over the next seven years, Cage and Cunningham increasingly loosened and eventually disregarded the need to connect their music and choreography. By 1953, most of Cunningham's dances were rehearsed in silence. The dancers learned to understand the internal rhythms of the choreography instead of listening for cues in the music, which was designed to hold its own regardless of the musical accompaniment.[121] This explains why Events could be performed to almost any type of sound—but music without a regular beat was always preferable.[122]

121. An exception is *Second Hand* (1969), for which Cage composed *Cheap Imitation* after Cunningham was refused permission to use a composition by Erik Satie; it has a one-to-one relationship between the music and movement. For a careful discussion of the significance of Satie to Cage and Cunningham, see Daniel Callahan, "The Gay Divorce of Music and Dance: Choreomusicality and the Early Works of Cage-Cunningham," *Journal of the American Musicological Society* vol. 71, no.2, 2018, pp.439–525.

The prototype for Cunningham's interest in disconnected simultaneity—like his interest in multi-directional stage space—is again often argued to be Cage's *Theatre Piece no. 1*. Yet the latter was improvisatory rather than rehearsed, and multiple performers did different things at different times, as opposed to separate components of the performance (dance, music, décor) running in parallel. *Theatre Piece no. 1* fragments the performative elements to produce a heterogeneity without unifying relationships. In Cunningham's best-known repertory productions, by contrast, an immediately recognizable "world" results from the convergence of choreography, music, set, and décor. Cunningham's work and *Theatre Piece*

122. This independence of choreography from music explains why Cunningham's works are so challenging for other dance companies to perform: ballet dancers have "spent so much time dancing to musical rhythms, when you take that away from them, they're lost and their rhythmic sense isn't strong enough to maintain something. So it becomes very lightweight. They start to skitter across the floor..." Chris Komar, oral history interview, 15 November 1993, p.15, Jerome Robbins Dance Division, NYPLPA.

No. 1 are both underpinned by a notion of collaboration as simultaneity, but the comparison ends there.

Over the decades, Cunningham's approach to collaboration was constant, but the caliber of the results was inconsistent. When working with visual artists, three main phases can be charted: the creative ferment of his collaborations with artistic directors Rauschenberg and Jasper Johns (1954 to 1980); a more muted period in the later 1970s and 1980s; and the high-profile commissions of the post-Cage era (1992–2009).[123] The musical choices were primarily the decision of Cage as the company's musical director, and later of Tudor and Takehisa Kosugi. Because these have been written about at length by music historians, I will touch upon this aspect of his collaborations only in passing.

As artistic director from 1954 to 1964, Rauschenberg specialized in highly inventive set designs in response to minimal prompts from Cunningham. In many ways, he continued the controlled anarchy approach of *Theatre Piece No. 1*. Much has been made of the freedom Rauschenberg was afforded—in his words, "a license to do anything"—even though he seems to have received more verbal cues from Cunningham than any subsequent artist.[124] Rauschenberg was an auto-didact. He hand-made his own costumes and sets, so there are no preparatory design sketches. His most memorable outfits are probably those for *Antic Meet* (1958), which include four swirling white dresses made of parachutes, a dishevelled fur coat, and a chair that was strapped to Cunningham's back. Equally untrained in lighting design, Rauschenberg regularly infuriated in-house technicians and triggered union conflicts.[125] His lighting system for *Winterbranch* (1963), for example, included non-theatrical headlights positioned in the wings and at the rear of the stage; these lit the dancers starkly and obliquely, and occasionally flashed into the audience, according to a schema that could be improvised while looking at the stage—or not.[126] In ten years, Rauschenberg only made

123. John Cage was music director until 1992, followed by David Tudor (to 1996), and Takehisa Kosugi. Rauschenberg was the first artistic director, followed by Jasper Johns, Mark Lancaster, and William Anastasi and Dove Bradshaw. Trevor Carlson gradually took on this role in the mid-1990s.

124. The phrase "license to do anything" comes from Rauschenberg's comments in Sally Banes, "Merce Cunningham's Story," in *Writing Dancing in the Age of Postmodernism*, Wesleyan University Press, 1994, pp.106–7.

125. Michelle Potter, "A License to Do Anything: Robert Rauschenberg and the Merce Cunningham Dance Company," *Dance Chronicle*, vol.16, no.1, pp.1–43.

126. The *Winterbranch* lighting concept specifies "off stage real worklites/ hall lights/ shop lights" and "handheld flashlites" (among others), to create a mood that is "shock, sharp, abrupt and bright (can be improvised either looking or not looking at the stage)." Robert Rauschenberg/Beverly Emmons, "Winterbranch – Concepts," 2012, Dance Capsule for Winterbranch, Lighting, item no. 14618.

one set that resembled a standard theatrical backcloth: the pointillist décor for *Summerspace*, which extended over the floor and onto the costumes, almost camouflaging the dancers.

For *Story*, Rauschenberg pioneered what he called "live décor." He made sets afresh for almost every performance, constructed from material he found in and around the theatre that day, as well as a prop to be picked up and moved around by the dancers on stage (during the section referred to as "Object"); this was only seen by the dancers thirty minutes before curtain. Costumes were a basic uniform of gold leotard and tights (for the women) and black tights and blue leotards (for the men), which the dancers customized each night by selecting clothes from duffel bags in the wings, filled with items that the artist had accumulated from thrift stores. **[Fig.32]** On the World Tour in 1964, Rauschenberg began to insert himself as part of the set. In London, for example, the artist worked on one of his combines onstage, also called *Story*, completing it on the fourth and final night. At Dartmouth, he and Alex Hay brought

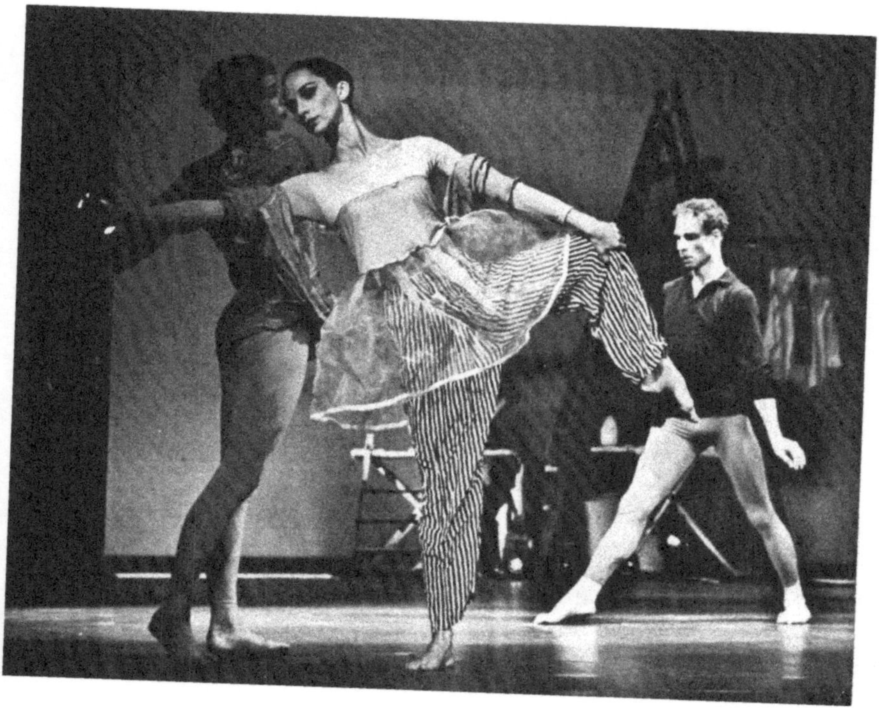

Fig.32
Story (1963). Carolyn Brown (center) and Merce Cunningham (right). Décor and costumes by Robert Rauschenberg. Photo: Douglas F. Jeffery.

two ironing boards on stage and proceeded to iron white shirts. This irritated some members of the company, as well as Cunningham himself, because it upstaged the dancers. This tension, in tandem with Rauschenberg's market success following the 1964 Venice Biennale, where he became the first American to win the Golden Lion, precipitated his departure from the company later that year.[127]

After Rauschenberg, Cunningham's collaborations took place within more clearly guarded parameters. Artists and musicians made their respective contributions but no longer drifted on stage. Rauschenberg, with typical jollity, later referred to his time with the company as "the most excruciating collaboration"—because "it was the most exciting, and most real, because nobody knew what anybody else was doing until it was too late."[128] While he thrived on the white-knuckle knife-edge, and welcomed the thrill of the unknown, Cunningham did not. By the time they parted ways, Rauschenberg had begun to experiment with his own performances, such as *Pelican* (1963), which featured Carolyn Brown wearing a parachute and moving around the stage on roller skates. It is telling that Rauschenberg referred to these forays into music and performance as "events," as if to underscore their experimental status.[129]

Johns took over the role of artistic director from 1967 to 1980, and adopted a new approach. Less smitten than Rauschenberg by the company's "gypsy-dance-troupe lifestyle," Johns invited a different artist—usually New York-based—to make décor for each piece, harking back to the tradition of Diaghilev and the Ballets Russes, who collaborated with numerous contemporary artists.[130] The most striking examples are hands-off (in terms of process) and obstructionist (in effect). For example, Frank Stella's movable set for *Scramble* (1968) occasionally obscures the choreography: six colored panels on steel frames are changed during every performance, depending

127. See Banes's interviews for her article, "Materials for an article on *Story* by Merce Cunningham," Merce Cunningham Dance Foundation Inc. Records, Additions, (S)*MGZMD 351, box 28, folder 2. The financial disparity between Rauschenberg and Cage and Cunningham became difficult for the older pair. At the bottom of one note on the running order of *Story*, Cunningham notes that Rauschenberg has finished the work he was doing on stage: "the painting finished—handsome, huge ($30,000?) on my time, too!" Cunningham, *Story* notebook, Merce Cunningham Dance Company Choreographic Records, (S) *MGZMD 295, box 19, folder 16.

128. Rauschenberg, in *The Collaborators: Cage, Cunningham, Rauschenberg*, St. Louis, Mo.: KETC Public Television, 1987.

129. Rauschenberg, in *The Collaborators: Cage, Cunningham, Rauschenberg*, St. Louis, Mo.: KETC Public Television, 1987.

130. Brown, in Klosty, *Merce Cunningham*, p.29.

on the order of the sections (decided by Cunningham), and moved around by the dancers.[131] **[Fig.33]** Robert Morris's set for *Canfield* (1969) comprises a vertical beam with ten lights; it sweeps across the stage, plunging the rest of the space into darkness. **[Fig.34]** Bruce Nauman literally phoned in the décor for *Tread* (1970): he requested twelve industrial fans facing the audience, which not only obstruct their view by rotating from side to side, but presumably chill the first rows of orchestra seating. **[Fig.35]** Johns's own designs tend to be minimal to the point of unremarkable: ombré costumes and scrims in gradations of grey.[132] The only notable exception is *Walkaround Time* (1968), for which he re-created Duchamp's *The Large Glass* (1915–23) as plastic sculptures; these, also, occasionally block the audience's view of the performers. **[Fig.36]**

131. Calvin Tomkins provides a wry account of the collaborative process leading to *Scramble* in 1967: artist Frank Stella visited the studio once, asked about the height of the tallest dancer and the size of the stage, and turned around designs for a movable set in less than two weeks. Calvin Tomkins, *The Bride and the Bachelors*, NY: Penguin, 1980, p.289.

132. Johns designed grey scrims for *Un jour ou deux* (1973) and *Exchange* (1976), and their accompanying ombré leotards. He was responsible for the costumes for *TV Rerun* (black and white leotards), *Landrover* and *Second Hand* (colored leotards). None of these works had décor. Johns designed grey leotards (which Morris covered in luminscent paint, but this quickly rubbed off) for *Canfield*, and flesh-coloured leotards for *Rainforest*.

Johns's former studio assistant Mark Lancaster took over as artistic director in 1975, and created minimal, largely unobtrusive sets for many repertory works, paired with bold-colored costumes.[133] His most notable décor was his first: a pair of dramatic, swirling, mustard-gold velvet curtains that tumble in elaborate baroque folds for *Sounddance* (1975). After 1984, the role of artistic director fell to Cage's close friend, conceptual artist William Anastasi and his partner, artist Dove Bradshaw, who at the time was making paintings with chemicals and natural materials (*Contingency Works*, 1984–2011). Their contributions were not particularly inspiring: the two artists were less proactive and adventurous as designers, reflecting their cautiousness as visual artists. Set designs were more conventional and lacked a confrontational dimension. Although Anastasi and Bradshaw were friends with Cunningham, there was little understanding about what could and couldn't be done on stage, leaving increased responsibility for the visual appearance of works to the aging Cunningham and Cage.[134]

133. See Alastair MacAulay, "Mark Lancaster (1938–2021), superlative designer for Merce Cunningham dance theatre, R.I.P.," 3 May 2021, https://www.alastairmacaulay.com/all-essays

134. Becofsky, oral history interview, 26 August 1997, p.108, Jerome Robbins Dance Division, NYPLPA.

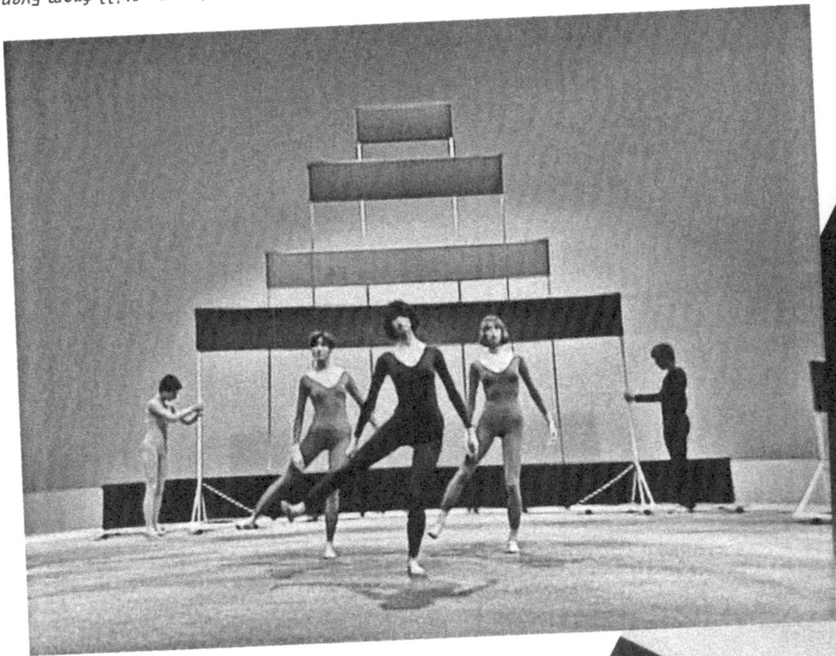

Fig.33 Still from *Event for Television* (1977). Directed by Merrill Brockway. Broadcast on WNET. Décor for *Scramble* (1967) by Frank Stella.

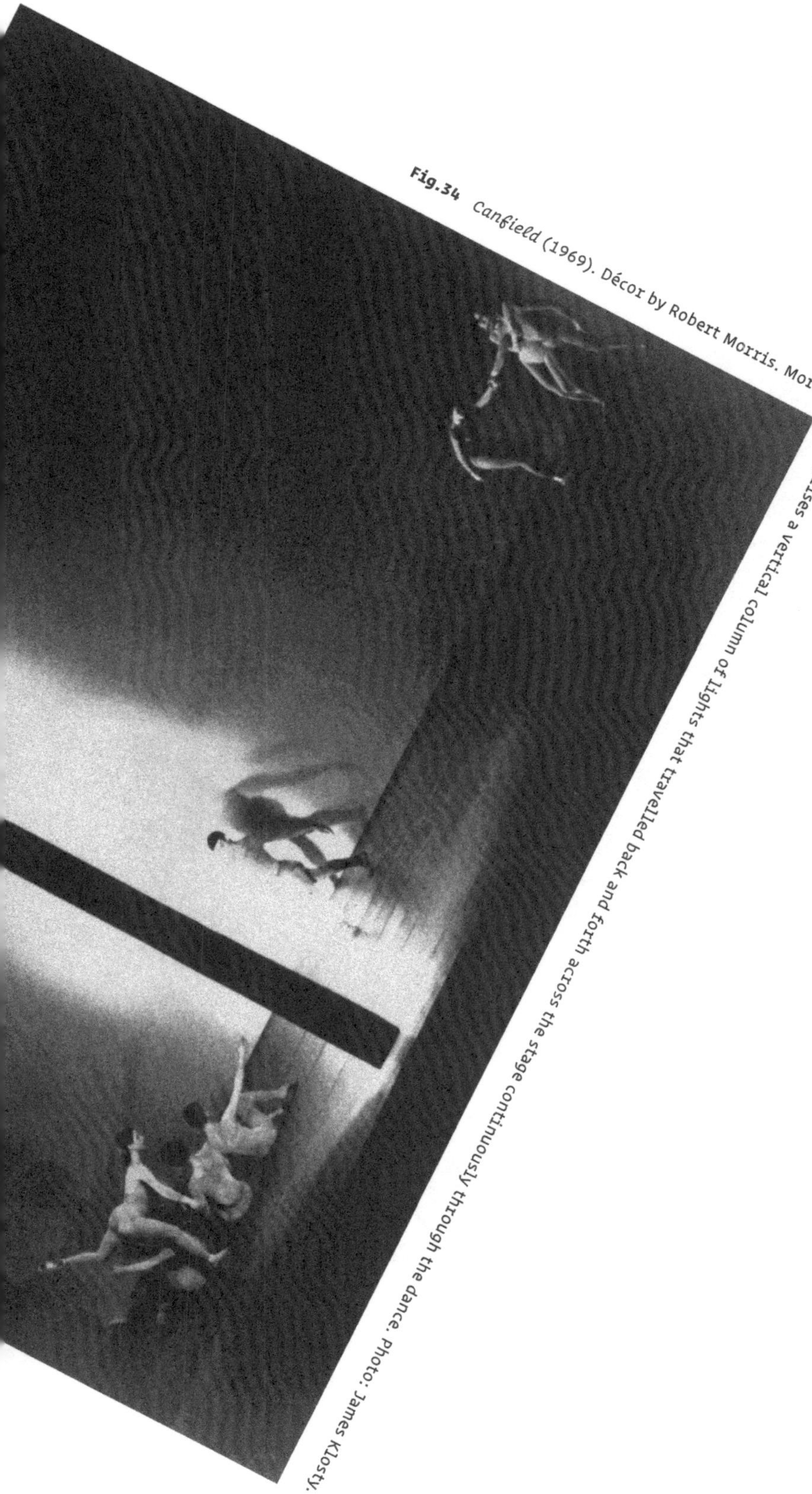

Fig.34 *Canfield* (1969). Décor by Robert Morris. Morris's set comprises a vertical column of lights that travelled back and forth across the stage continuously through the dance. Photo: James Klosty.

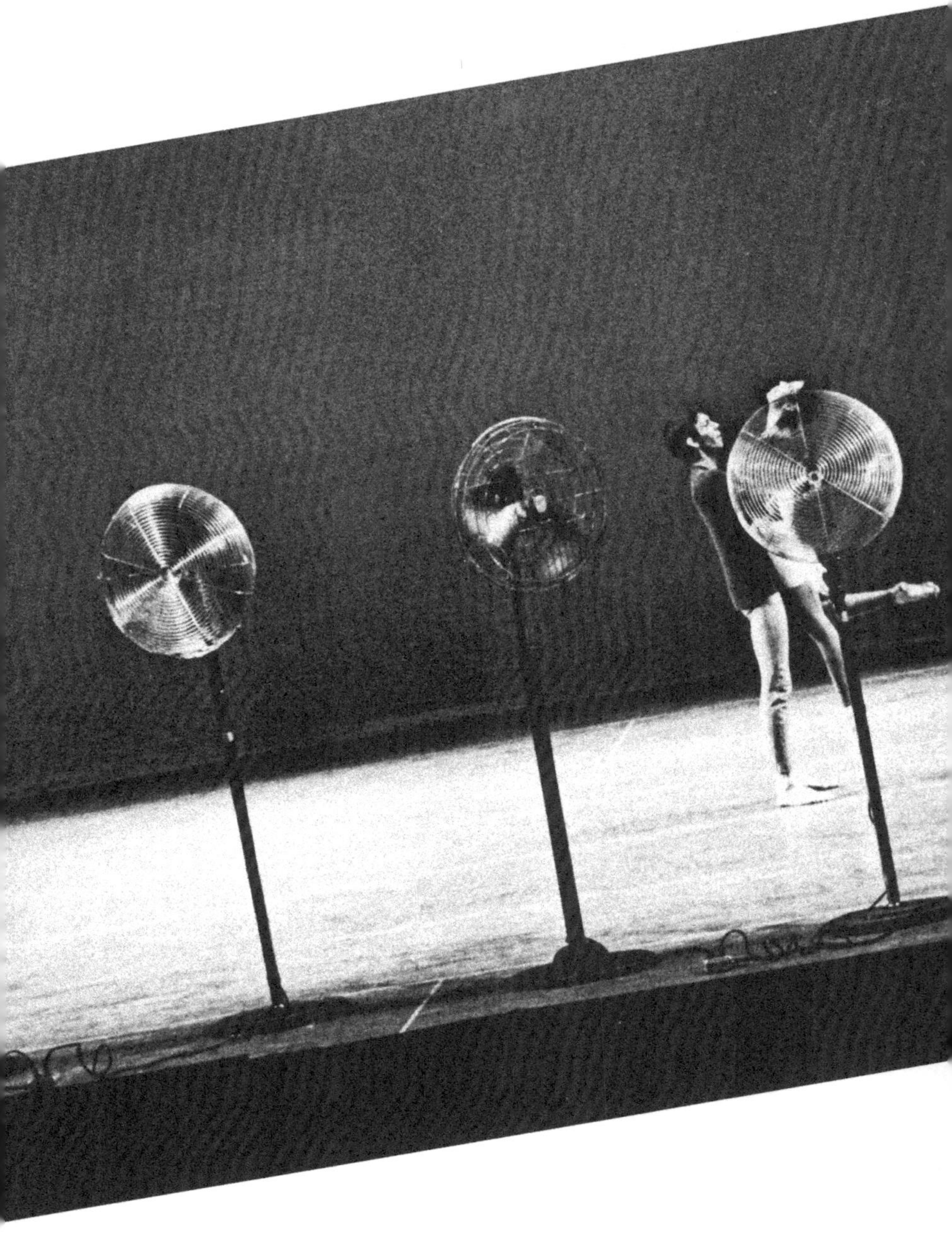

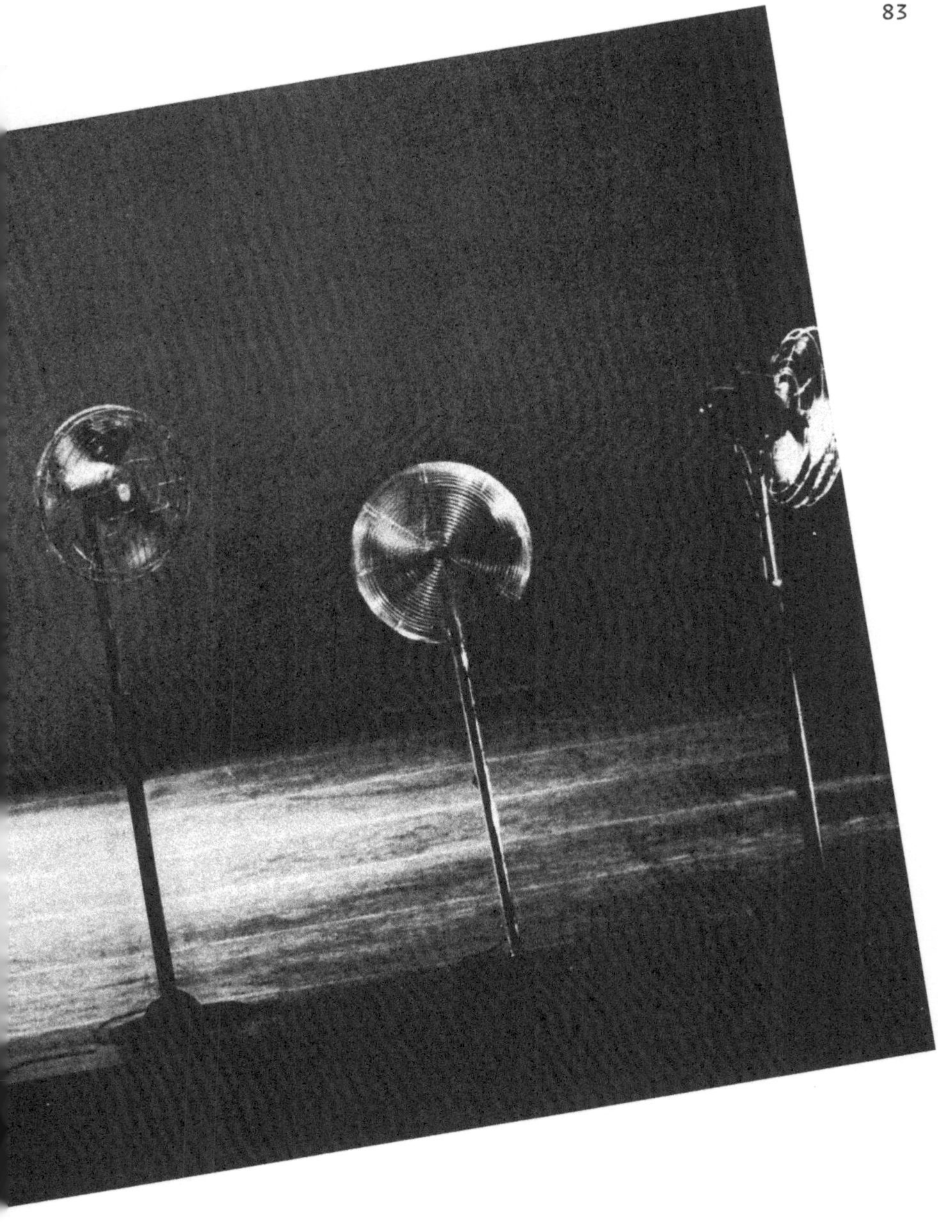

Fig.35
Tread (1969). Décor by Bruce Nauman. Ten large industrial fans are aligned in a row across the front of the stage, alternately stationary and turning from side to side, and blowing out into the audience. Photo: James Klosty.

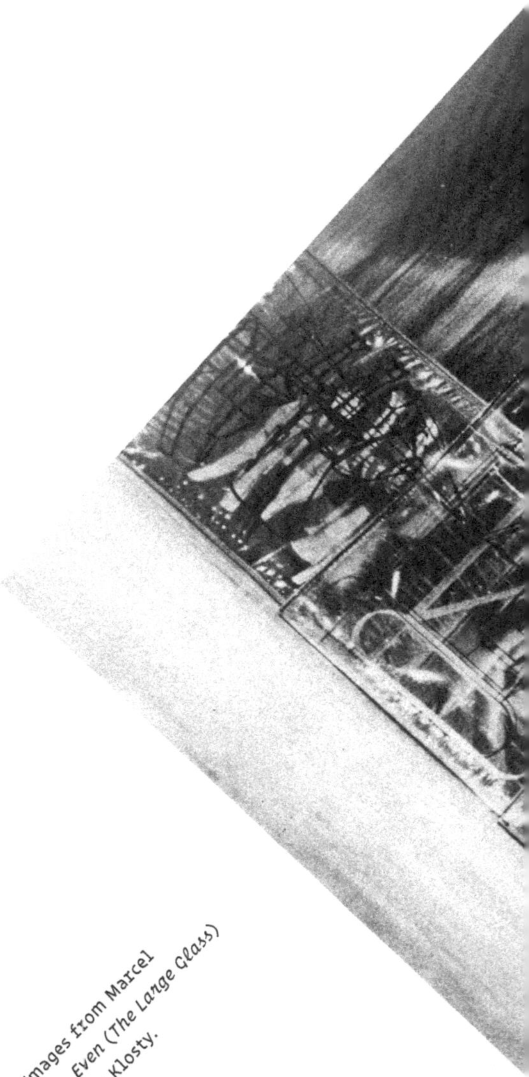

Fig.36
Walkaround Time (1968). Décor by Jasper Johns. Images from Marcel Duchamp's *The Bride Stripped Bare by Her Bachelors, Even* (*The Large Glass*) (1915–23), silk-screened onto clear vinyl. Photo: James Klosty.

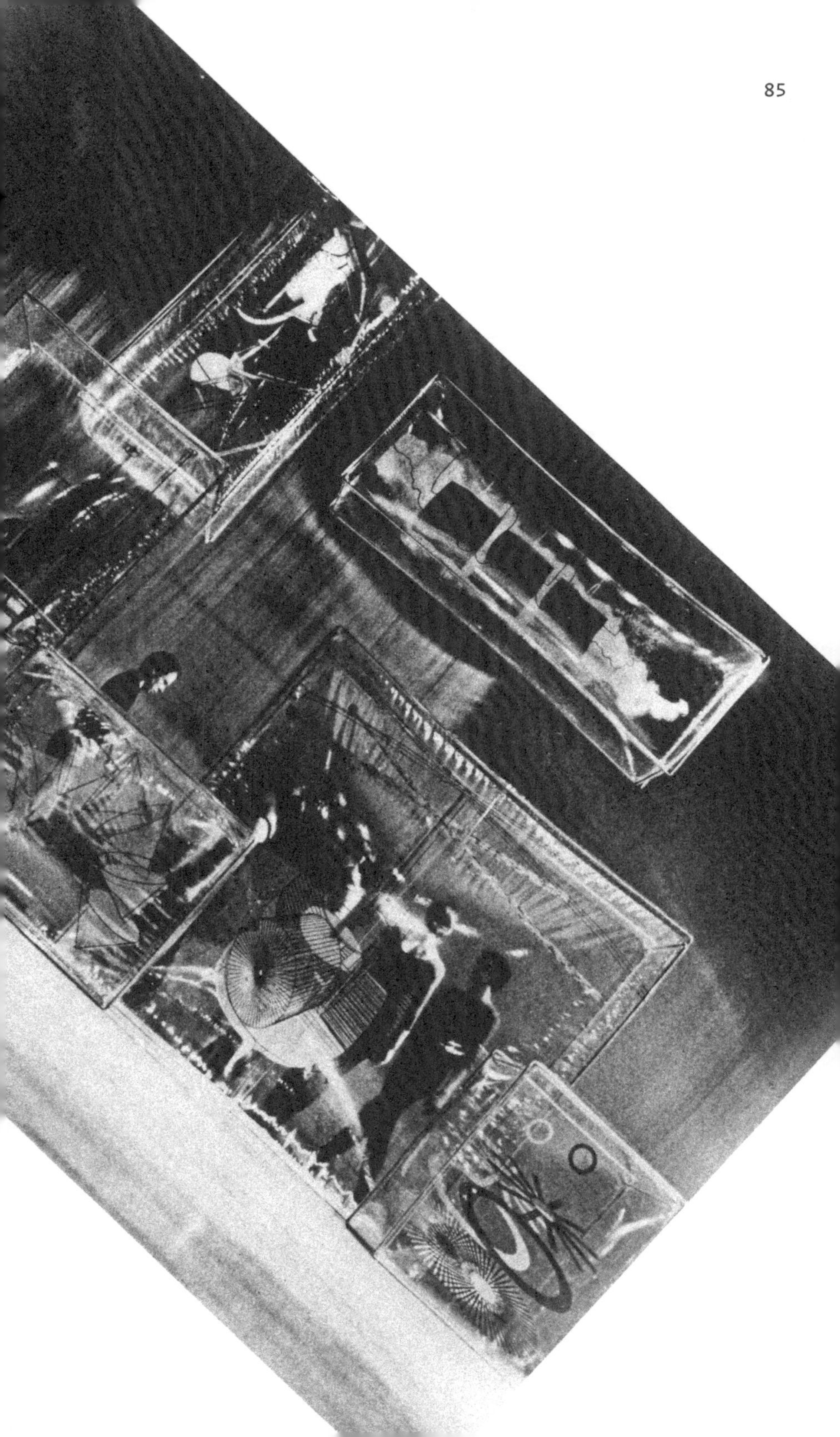

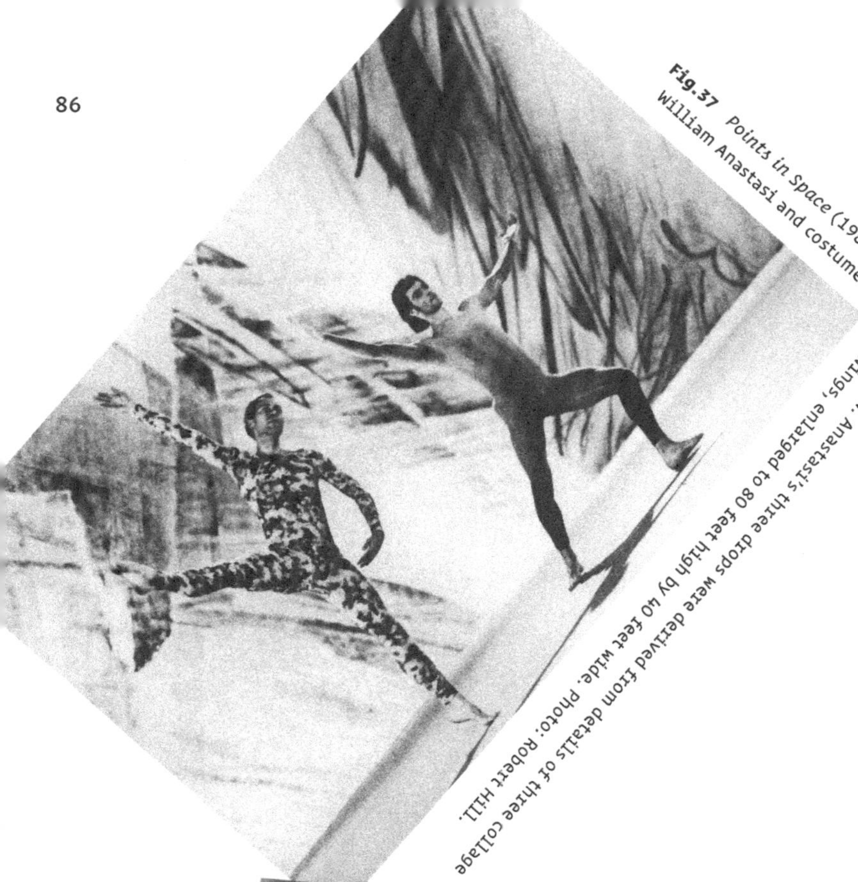

Fig.37 *Points in Space* (1987). Décor by William Anastasi and costumes by Dove Bradshaw. Anastasi's three drops were derived from details of three collage drawings, enlarged to 80 feet high by 40 feet wide. Photo: Robert Hill.

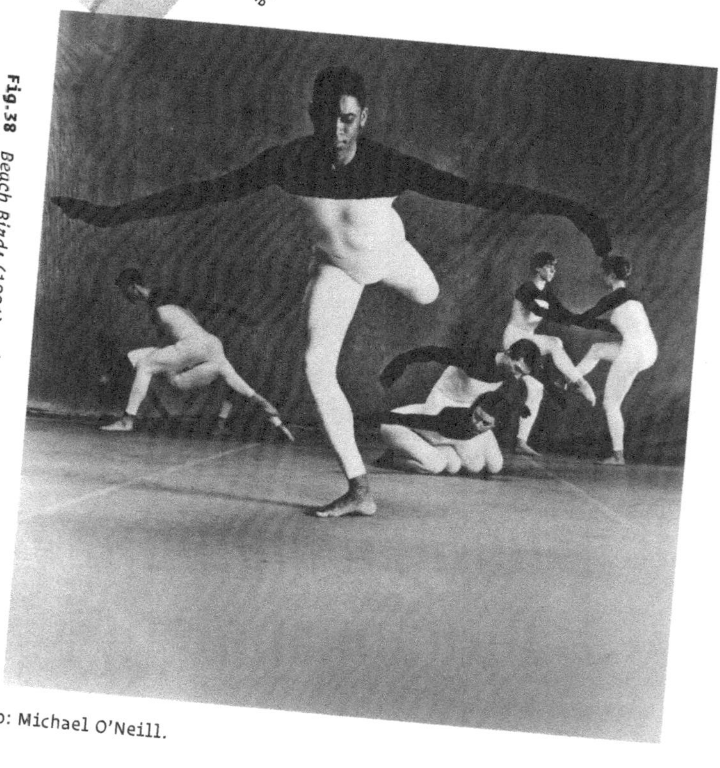

Fig.38 *Beach Birds* (1991). Décor and costumes by Marsha Skinner. Photo: Michael O'Neill.

Anastasi and Bradshaw tended to scale up small works on paper for a scrim or drop, usually with a black velour curtain behind, creating a self-contained world for the dance (rather than one that intruded into the theatre space, or exposed the back of the stage). For *Points in Space* (1987), for example, Anastasi enlarged a mixed-media abstraction to a 40' x 80' panoramic backcloth, and Bradshaw made two matching sets of costumes (one ombré, one tachiste). **[Fig.37]** Bradshaw's sets for *Fabrications* (also 1987) again enlarged a mixed-media work in oil, china marker, graphite and colored pencil. The aesthetic is arty but polite: a complete U-turn away from the experiments of the 1960s while also avoiding signal artistic developments of the 1980s (e.g., appropriation, remediation, abjection). Anastasi and Bradshaw's efforts are conspicuously less autonomous as artistic statements than previous collaborations, and appear subservient to the choreography—a quality that also characterizes their choice of guest artists. Cunningham's most distinctive collaboration of this period is with Marsha Skinner, whose black-and-white unitards and naturalistic lighting-as-set for *Beach Birds* (1991) are immediately recognizable in their classicism—much like Cunningham's choreography by this point.[135] **[Fig.38]**

Cage had been responsible for inviting artistic directors to join the company. After his death in 1992, and Tudor's in 1996, executive director Trevor Carlson sought to refresh the company's image by seeking out new, high-profile collaborations. In 1996, fashion designer Rei Kawakubo, founder of Comme des Garçons, was invited to design costumes and sets for a new production. The decision was surprising. Cunningham had strict limitations on costume and had never collaborated with fashion designers. As Brown explains: "the nearly inflexible rule was: body unencumbered, body visible."[136] Clothes from Kawakubo's spring 1997 collection were adapted as the costumes for Cunningham's *Scenario* that year. Down-padded "beans" and "U" shapes were added to dresses and unitards, forming irregular bulges on the dancers' hips, backs, chests and shoulders. This was the first time that Cunningham had allowed a designer to distort the dancers' bodies, and some of the padded "beans" needed to be adjusted when he discovered that they restricted movement.

135. *Beach Birds* contains stylized animal gestures (flutters and ripples through extended arms and legs) and abundant ballet positions: legs in turned-out third and first position, pliés, sautés, and arabesques. Thanks to Flora Brandl for these observations.

136. Brown, *Chance and Circumstance*, p.147.

As a result, *Scenario* was the only work in the company's repertoire that needed to be rehearsed in costume. **[Fig.39]** As anticipated, the collaboration generated media coverage, but the work was retired from repertory in 1999; excerpts survived as *Scenario MinEvent*, programmed alongside the iPod collaboration *EyeSpace* in 2006.

The example of Comme des Garçons points to the new role of collaboration from the late 1990s onwards, which was increasingly in the service of marketing. These collaborations can be viewed as arranged marriages for publicity, designed to boost media coverage and ticket sales: a juxtaposition of prestigious brands rather than a meeting of minds or artistic temperaments. They also held strong appeal as fundraising opportunities. The minutes of the Board of Directors meeting on 19 September 1996, for example, note that "Rei Kawakubo is one of the wealthiest women in Japan," and that her collaboration with Cunningham would be announced through a cocktail reception in Paris that could double as a "Special Cultivation Event."[137]

The Events, meanwhile, were reoriented to take place largely with *local* collaborators: inviting a musician to provide the soundtrack, and a visual artist to supply a work of art for the décor, who were based in the city of the performance. Each Event could therefore be claimed as unique not just in its sequence of excerpts but also in musical accompaniment and décor. At the Barbican Center in London in 2004, for example, six different musicians and six different artists accompanied Events on six consecutive evenings, and the series was billed as "six unique evenings [...] six totally new shows."[138] What is notable here is the speed of turnover: a new visual artist and a new musician *every evening*, rather than the longer-term relationships that characterize repertory productions.

The interest in big-name partners continued into the 2000s, even if the results often left something to be desired. *Nearly Ninety* (2009), for example, featured costumes by fashion designer Romeo Gigli and music by Takehisa Kosugi, John Paul Jones, and the noise rock band Sonic Youth. The décor, a grandiose tower by Italian

137. 19 September 1996, Board of Directors' Minutes, Merce Cunningham Dance Foundation Inc. Records, Additions, (S)*MGZMD 351, box 14, folder 4.

138. Press release, "Merce Cunningham Dance Company's Events," Barbican Center, London, 2004. The visual artists were Darren Almond, David Batchelor, Marc Camille Chaimowicz, Enrico David, Richard Hamilton and Roger Hiorns; the musicians were John Paul Jones, John King, Takehisa Kosugi, Kaffe Mathews, Steve Montague, Scanner and Philip Selway. The line-up is typical in its inclusion of just one female artist.

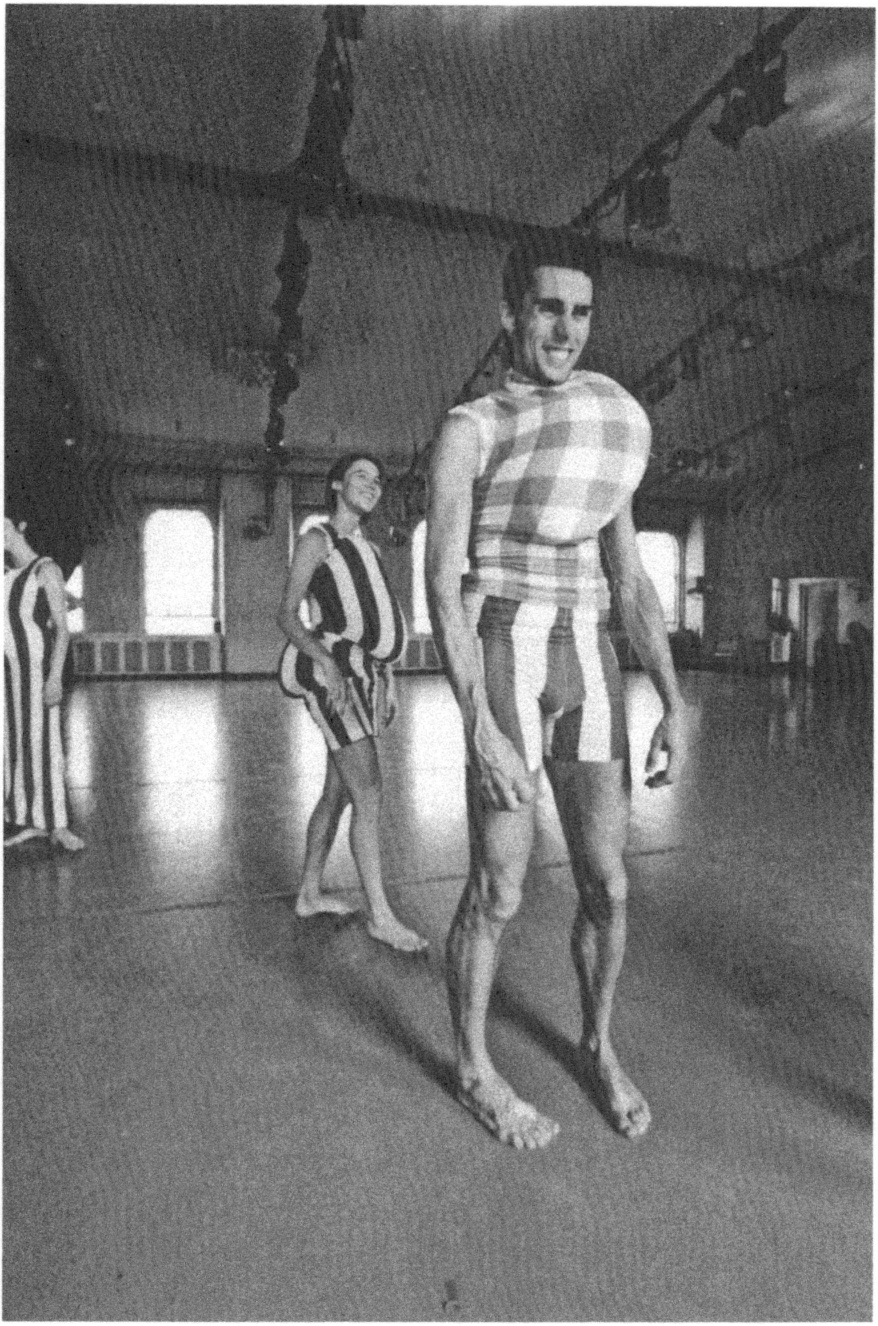

Fig.39

Dancers Jean Freebury and Matthew Mohr rehearsing at Westbeth in Rei Kawakubo costumes for *Scenario* (1997). Photo: Timothy Greenfield-Sanders.

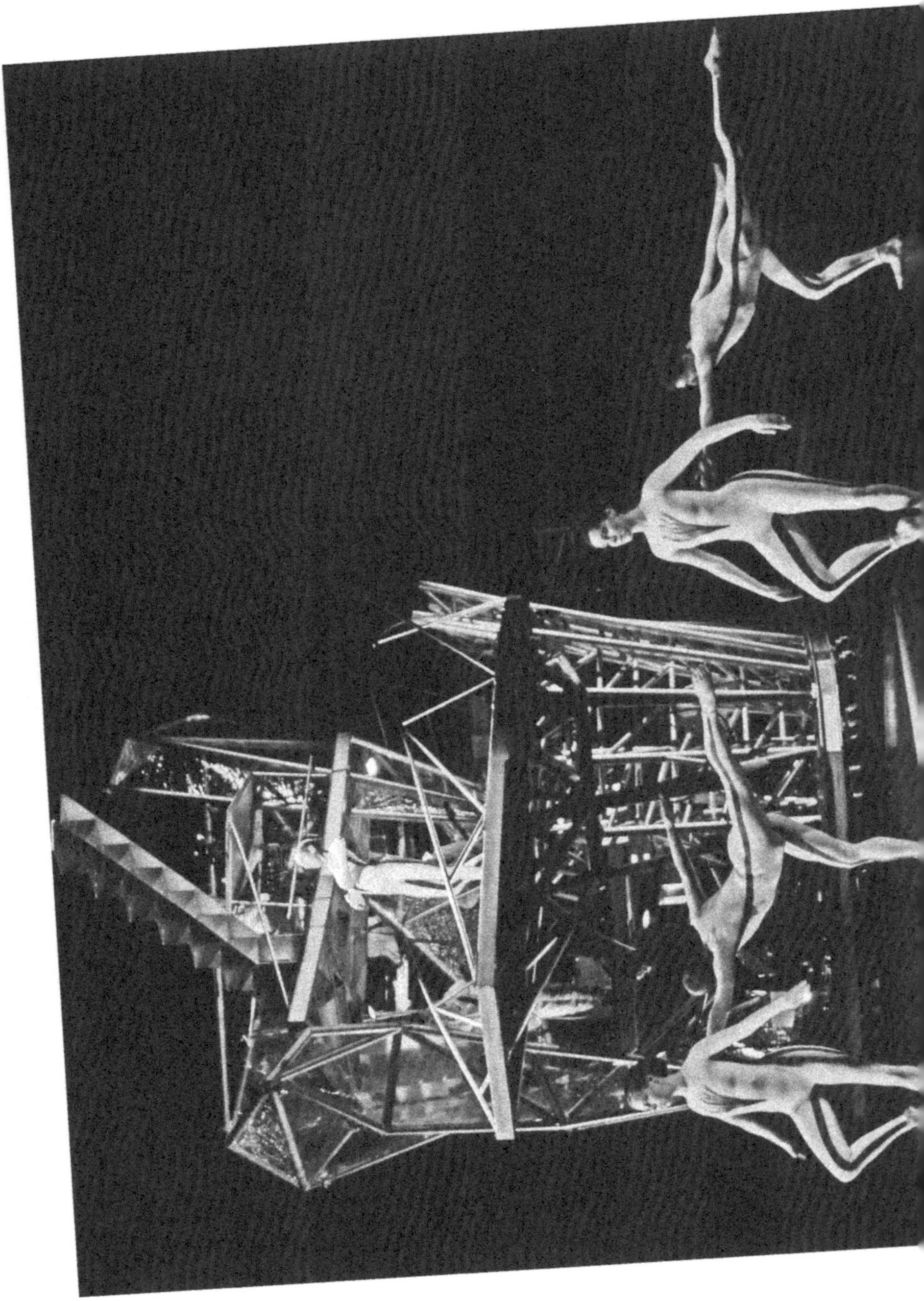

Fig.40
Nearly Ninety (2009). Décor by Benedetta Tagliabue and costumes by Romeo Gigli. Photo: Anna Finke.

architect Benedetta Tagliabue, left very little stage space for the dancers, was too heavy to tour, and required extra insurance for the stagehands. **[Fig.40]** A second, stripped-down version was rapidly put into place for touring —without the cumbersome set, the Gigli costumes, or Sonic Youth (*Nearly Ninety-2*). Celebrity collaboration was mobilized to grab attention and funding, but could be jettisoned when it came down to the practicalities of touring. As the Events demonstrated, over and again, for Cunningham the choreography was primary, not the *gesamtkunstwerk* (the harmonious fusion of dance, music, and poetry in the manner of Greek tragedy).[139] Cunningham's approach is more disintegrated: a decentered stage space, the removal of narrative, décor that could block a clear view of the dancers, and musical accompaniment that might exist in a completely different tonal register to the choreography.[140] Comparing Cunningham to the Ballets Russes, David Vaughan pointed out that the latter formed an "integrated spectacle," while Cunningham's is always "disintegrated."[141] Yet the difference is not so clear: in Cunningham's best-known works, the choreography, sets, costumes, and music nevertheless cohere against the odds to produce a distinctive unity. The average viewer would never know that these pieces are the result of fortuitous encounter rather than years of exchange and dialogue.[142]

The forty-year collaboration between Martha Graham (Cunningham's former employer) and sculptor Isamu Noguchi stands as a contrasting model of long-term collaboration and exchange between a choreographer and visual artist. Noguchi responded to ideas put forward by her chief composer Louis Horst, while Graham

139. Richard Wagner, *The Artwork of the Future, and Other Works*, Lincoln: University of Nebraska Press, 1993.

140. The two most idiosyncratic examples of musical accompaniment in the Cunningham repertoire both stretch the definition of "music," and either entertain or annoy, depending on your disposition. The first is for *How to Pass, Kick, Fall and Run*, where Cage and another performer sit at a table on stage, drinking champagne and reading Cage's *Indeterminacy*, an anthology of one-minute stories. The second is Pauline Oliveros's score for *Canfield*, *In Memoriam: Nikola Tesla, Cosmic Engineer* (1969): at least four performers wander around the venue and communicate with each other over a wireless system, exploring acoustic phenomena with a range of objects including a cap pistol, bugle, and slide whistle.

141. David Vaughan, "Diaghilev/Cunningham," *Art Journal*, Winter 1974–75, Vol.34, No.2, p.138.

142. It's telling to compare the number of repertory dances that Cunningham choreographed (180) with the number that have been turned into "dance capsules" (86), the Merce Cunningham Trust's remarkable digital archive that has been central to this research: https://dancecapsules.mercecunningham.org/

would speak to Noguchi about problems she was having with the choreography, which he would attempt to resolve through props and costumes.[143] The long-term relationship between Graham and Noguchi provides a stark foil to the lack of communication between Cunningham and his collaborators, which might best be described as "parallel play," the term that child psychologists use to describe the developmental stage in which toddlers play alongside each other without interacting.[144] Each contributor focuses on their own "toy," happy to work alongside others as long as they don't interfere with their own particular objects.

Parallel play is a suggestive descriptor of Cunningham's approach to collaboration, which worked best in the 1960s, when his collaborators were drawn from a small group of like-minded artists—initially from Black Mountain College, and then from downtown New York. It is not coincidental that many of them were also white and gay.[145] The artists shared a place and time, an aesthetic orientation, and a certain set of formal preoccupations, including an interest in dismantling perspective and a fixed point of view. Formal strategies like silence and neutrality have been read as metaphors for the closet—the only viable option for artists of their generation—so it is tempting to refer to these collaborations as queer, even if the collaborators were not all homosexual.[146]

It is striking how little was discussed. Reflecting in 1987 on his collaboration with Cunningham, composer Morton Feldman acknowledged that music and dance "could be independent as long as everybody is agreeing

143. See Dore Ashton, *Noguchi East and West*, Berkeley: University of California Press, 1992, pp.58–60. Graham recalled: "When I brooded on what I felt was the unresolved problem of representing Medea flying to return to her father the Sun, Isamu devised a dress worked from brilliant pieces of bronze wire that became my garment as Medea moved with me across the stage in my chariot of flames." (p.58).

144. Parallel play was put forward by sociologist Mildred Parten in 1933 as the first of three developmental stages, the second being "social play" (sharing and playing) and the third "cooperative play" (complementary roles; shared purpose). Parten, "Social play among preschool children," *The Journal of Abnormal and Social Psychology*, 1933, vol.28, no.2, pp.136–147. Thanks to Jonah Westerman for this analogy.

145. See Moira Roth's comments on "the homosexuality and bisexuality permissable and even common among the new aesthetic group." Roth, "The Aesthetic of Indifference," *Artforum*, November 1977, p.49. She is referring to Duchamp, Cage, Cunningham, Rauschenberg and Johns.

146. See for example Jonathan Katz, "Lovers and Divers: Interpictorial Dialog in the Work of Jasper Johns and Robert Rauschenberg," *Frauen Kunst Wissenschaft* vol. 25, 1998, pp.16–31; "John Cage's Queer Silence; or, how to avoid making matters worse," *GLQ: A Journal of Gay and Lesbian Studies*, vol.5, no.2, 1999, pp.231–52; Susan Leigh Foster, "Closets Full of Dances: Modern Dance's Performance of Masculinity and Sexuality," in Jane Desmond (ed.), *Dancing Desires: Choreographing Sexualities On And Off The Stage*, Wisconsin: University of Wisconsin Press, 2001, pp.147–207; Bill T. Jones, *Story/Time: The Life of an Idea*, Princeton University Press, 2014; Noland, *Merce Cunningham: After the Arbitrary*, chapter 7.

with each other."[147] Cunningham's "safety net" (Feldman again) was that everyone shared a similar sense of what was appropriate. But this tacit consensus was carefully circumscribed—not unlike Cunningham's limited experiments with indeterminacy. During the same symposium, composer Christian Wolff described two painful incidents in which he inadvertently transgressed Cunningham's tacit rules of collaboration: an Event at Westbeth in which he played music that was rhythmic (and thus threw off the dancers, who couldn't tune it out) and an Event at the Joyce in which he played political folk songs, including Woodie Guthrie, just as Cunningham began a solo. His choices were seen as having broken an aesthetic contract ("when it was over, nobody would talk to me").[148] Parallel play only worked if everyone subscribed to the same unspoken aesthetic consensus.

By the later 1990s, the company's collaborations had very little to do with a shared sensibility, but the implicit rule of parallel play remained in force. Event collaborations in particular seem to be based on matters of scale and availability more than aesthetic consistency. The invited visual artists and musicians were removed from Cunningham's milieu both generationally and geographically, but this was viewed by the company as an asset when marketing tours to local audiences. (In the words of Carlson, "the Event alone is not as sexy as an Event with a local artist and musician, i.e., a new collaborator.")[149] Carlson visited artists and gallerists, saw works in storage, and discussed options with Cunningham; pre-existing works were selected on the basis of their size and ability to hold their own on stage.

The idea of collaboration, then, changes significantly from the frisson of unspoken (closeted) agreement in the 1950s and 1960s. By the 1980s, the model was the unadventurous comfort of platonic friendship (Anastasi and Bradshaw) while the final decade and a half was marked by expediency—a series of one-night stands rather than long-term affairs. The relationship with Charles Atlas stands out as an obvious exception to this approach. At first glance,

147. Morton Feldman, in "Merce Cunningham and the New Dance" (1987), sound recording at Jerome Robbins Dance Division, NYPLPA, *MGZTC 3-1193, tapes 7 to 9.

148. For Wolff the incident epitomized the larger problem of the company's detachment from politics and the world around them. Christian Wolff, in "Merce Cunningham and the New Dance" (1987), sound recording at Jerome Robbins Dance Division, NYPLPA, *MGZTC 3-1193, tapes 7 to 9.

149. Carlson, interview with the author, via Skype, 22 February 2018. In a follow-up interview, Carlson described how "a local visual artist really sweetens the pot" when trying to put together a tour. Carlson, interview with the author, via Skype, 14 December 2018.

 Cunningham's collaboration with Atlas seems to be the only one that fits the conventional understanding of this term, as two creatives in close dialogue. They worked together on all levels of VideoDance production: physically setting up the cameras, deck, and monitor after the morning class; grabbing three hours of filming; de-installing miles of cable and equipment before the afternoon class. They worked out the angles of shots and established how to deal with cuts. They both handled the camera equipment—Cunningham even ended up as a second cameraman because the job demanded close knowledge of the dance and when to move to the next shot. Finally, during editing, Cunningham sat alongside Atlas, looking at every take to establish which was the best.[150]

Yet this relationship, framed by Atlas as a collaboration—indeed, as the ultimate collaboration—isn't acknowledged as such by Cunningham. For example, in Nam June Paik and Shigeko Kubota's video *Merce by Merce by Paik* (1977), the first half of the twenty-nine-minute work comprises *Blue Studio: Five Segments*, a VideoDance made by Atlas and Cunningham for WNET/TB Lab in 1975. Yet Atlas isn't credited in the title, which should properly read *Merce by Atlas by Paik*. (Kubota is equally uncredited, reflecting the marginalized status of female partners at that time.) One way to understand this difference is generational: Cunningham was thirty years Atlas's senior, and their relationship was one of employer and employee. Although Atlas arrived at the company as an attractive twenty-one-year-old (by his own admission, as a "kid") and felt that Cunningham treated him like "an equal", he clearly did not have the same status as the other visual artists in that milieu.

On the other hand, dancer Carolyn Brown, just eight years younger, endured the choreographer's poor communication for eighteen years. At several points in her autobiography, Brown recalls taking Cunningham to task over his awkward social skills, antisocial disposition, and refusal to take directorial responsibility

150. "I really remember the third piece Merce and I did in 1976, *Squaregame Video*. Merce sat with me in the back, where I was editing, and we went over every take because I couldn't tell what a good performance was." Atlas, in Brooks, "Interview with Charles Atlas, Rashaun Mitchell, and Silas Riener," p.229.

over the dancers, such as informing them about upcoming performances and tours.[151] Cunningham's first student Marianne Preger-Simon, later turned psychotherapist, recalls that he was so averse to confrontation that he couldn't even collect fees for his classes; she describes his "dark moods" and attributes them to his closeted status as well as lack of public recognition.[152] The differences here are striking, pointing both to gender differences and the uneasy hierarchy between choreographer and dancer. Cunningham never viewed his working relationship with dancers as a collaboration. His private thoughts remained inaccessible to them, and they had no idea what he thought of their performances. As Douglas Dunn recalls, "He took care of his own emotional life by working his butt off all day every day. And not revealing all the stuff he didn't want to reveal, which was ninety percent of his life."[153]

Accordingly, company hierarchy was not perceived as incompatible with Cage and Cunningham's philosophy of egalitarian creative coexistence: not to impinge in any way upon the output of another artist. Cage parses this in terms of the Zen Buddhist principle of "nonobstruction"—a principle of nonrelation and non-derangement, separate but together, independent yet sharing time and space. There should be no special effort of give-and-take between artists, nothing that would lead to making art or music in a different way—only, in Cage's words, "a willingness to have your work experienced at the same time other work is

151. Brown, *Chance and Circumstance*, p.80, 316, 328. Brown notes how Valda Setterfield was an exception and seemed comfortable discussing anything with Cunningham (Setterfield corroborated this in a conversation with the author, New York, 14 March 2018). Karol Armitage, who danced with Cunningham between 1976 and 1981, recalled that "being in the company was a cold experience. Merce did not talk to anyone, ever. He gave no corrections, no communication. He'd walk in the room, say, 'We are doing this piece,' turn on the stopwatch and comment at the end, 'Two seconds too slow,' or, 'Two seconds too fast.'" Armitage, in Lyndsey Winship, "'He said two things to me in five years. And one was thanks for the cheese' – Merce Cunningham remembered," *The Guardian*, 15 April 2019.

152. Marianne Preger-Simon, *Dancing with Merce Cunningham*, Gainesville: University Press of Florida, 2019, pp.65, 83. She went around the class on his behalf, collecting fees. Her suggestion that Cunningham's dark moods relate to his being closeted is retrospective, since during the 1950s his dancers had no knowledge of his romantic partnership with Cage: "Most of us dancers were somewhat in love with him, myself included, having little comprehension of his homosexuality; neither were many of us aware of his romantic relationship with John Cage. (I didn't become aware of their intimate partnership until after leaving the company, when gay relationships became comfortably public.)" (p.66)

153. Douglas Dunn, interview with the author, New York, 11 April 2018.

experienced."[154] Yet the dancers (mostly women) are not regarded as equals, only the musicians and artists (mostly men).[155]

154. "Interpenetration and nonobstruction, those are the two great principles." Cage, "On Collaboration in Art: A Conversation with David Shapiro," *RES: Anthropology and Aesthetics*, no.10, Autumn 1985, p.112.

155. This prioritization can be seen in a page of Cunningham's notebooks from 1965 that breaks down the weekly cost of running the company ($2000). After Cunningham is paid at $160 per week (plus tax), it is telling that the next three employees are musicians rather than dancers: John Cage, David Tudor, and Ishinayagi, each at $150 per week. The dancers are paid less: $135 (Carolyn Brown, Viola Farber) and $120 (Barbara Lloyd, Sandra Neels, Gus Solomons, and Albert Reed). Merce Cunningham Dance Company Choreographic Records, (S)*MGZMD 295, box 19, folder 16, *Story* notebook.

Cunningham's enthusiasm for horizontal collaboration was less reliant on Zen Buddhism and more often dressed up as a politics of egalitarianism: "in a way, it's a political move. It's saying that one person isn't better than somebody else."[156] This was most convincing when collaboration was framed as a motor for aesthetic novelty and vitality: "the possibility of discovery through the coming together of supposedly disparate things [...] disparate things brought together can produce an energy and a life that might otherwise be missed."[157] When this worked out, the results created a distinctive and unified whole, and these are the so-called masterpieces: *Summerspace*, *Rainforest*, *Walkaround Time*, *Sounddance, Beach Birds,* and *Biped*, among others. When the choreography was sabotaged by music, décor, or costumes that didn't quite work, this wasn't necessarily a disaster. The dance could always be saved through reincarnation in Events.

156. Cunningham, in "Interview with Merce Cunningham," *Ballet Review*, v.27, no.4, Winter 1999, p.22. Cage makes the same equation between collaboration and democracy, in Cage, "On Collaboration in Art: A Conversation with David Shapiro," p.107.

It is therefore in the Events where the Cunningham experiment is most fully realized: the choreography in its independence and integrity is kept alive because of its perpetual recombinatory possibilities with new music and décor. The vitality of new juxtapositions and simultaneities was sustained through a model of collaboration as parallel play. Whether the Events are the most aesthetically satisfying manifestation of Cunningham's output is less clear, but they are where his process and principles are most visible. Rather than the production of *the great work*, the Events make public the *ongoing work* of a choreographic practice.

157. Cunningham, "Collaborating with Visual Artists" (1983), unpublished essay, https://www.mercecunningham.org/the-work/writings/collaborating-with-visual-artists/. See also his observation, in the same essay, that what concerns him is "how to keep [dance] alive in whatever form it takes, on the stage, throughout a basketball court, in a hall surrounded by paintings and sculptures or on a television or movie screen."

Contingency

Over and again, flexibility emerges as a key term in the history of Events: their ability to serve as a vehicle for performing in different spaces, stages, and climates, with different numbers of dancers, solving the problem of how to present Cunningham's work to an audience regardless of a venue's size or suitability. Events enabled Cunningham to make a performance in an amphitheatre, a gymnasium, an inflatable theatre, a television studio or whatever space was made available. In the early years, Events reflected the company's own adaptability, as it would show up to a venue not fully knowing what the circumstances would be. Information was not always shared ahead of time, and occasionally turned out to be inaccurate. In 1966, Cunningham described how they might only see the venue on the morning of the performance, and have to make a decision on the spot as to what would work best in the space:

> When we enter a strange theatre in the morning with a performance to give in the evening, the first anticipation is for a look at the stage. What's it like? Large or small? Everyone is delighted if it is large, spacious and equipped, grimly accepting if it is "another one of those." The next look is at the floor, what our feet have to withstand [...]

> After this stagework, I have to check the program that is scheduled to be presented, to know if it actually can be performed on that stage. Some dances will not function at all on small stages, and although we have have tried to receive information ahead of time, the information sent may not be accurated, or as with Prague, we were not able to get any, and the stated program must be unstated.[158]

On arriving in Mannheim in 1964, the company encountered a stage whose floor was "extremely bad, full of small tacks and splintery."[159] The stagehands refused to do anything about it, so the company spent the afternoon on hands and knees, systematically clearing the boards until they were safe to dance upon.

By the late 1990s, however, such adaptability became a way to accommodate a less extreme set of variables: the unforeseen encounter between Cunningham's choreography, a musician, and a visual artist. New lighting, décor, music, and costumes would penetrate the choreography and colour its mood, delivering a constellation whose ostensible (but in fact inevitable) uniqueness was catnip for producers and programmers. Any uncertainty about the results—the extent to which a composer's performance would resonate with the dance excerpts, for example, or how effectively an artist's work would function as a décor—was subsumed by the thrill of attending a one-off, never-to-be-repeated combination. This highly visible but failsafe embrace of contingency as a marketing device is qualitatively different to the unpredictability experienced by the company in the 1960s and 1970s, when the venue itself—and what could be performed there—was an unknown quantity. In the company's final years, the spontaneity of decision-making that Cunningham described in 1966 was foreclosed entirely: a week of technical set-up was required prior to an Event, together with a minimum dancing area of forty by thirty feet.[160]

How this shift took place is in part a conventional tale of the

158. Cunningham, notes for Lecture-Demonstration at Moderna Museet, Stockholm, 5 Nov 1966, p.2, in Merce Cunningham Dance Foundation Inc. Records, Additions, (S)*MGZMD 351, box 29, folder 3.

159. Cunningham, notes for Lecture-Demonstration at Moderna Museet, Stockholm, 5 Nov 1966, p.2.

160. See the draft contract for the Events at Mercat de les Flors in Barcelona, November 2009, in Merce Cunningham Dance Foundation Inc. Records, Additions, (S)*MGZMD 351, box 146, folder 4. For the minimum dancing area, see the "Event Technical Rider," revised 11/20/07, p.4, same folder.

inverse relationship between financial stability and aesthetic risk, and in part a story of the company's relationship with the union, the American Guild of Musicians and Artists (AGMA). Cunningham Dance Foundation, as it was known from 1964 onwards, was one of the first modern dance companies to join AGMA, once membership became a requirement for receiving funding from the National Endowment for the Arts.[161] In her autobiography, Carolyn Brown repeatedly notes her unease at having to sign a union contract with AGMA in order to perform in certain venues. Along with dancers from Alvin Ailey, Alwin Nikolais, and Paul Taylor, Brown signed a letter to AGMA in 1967, protesting its insistence that modern dance companies join the organization.[162] **[Fig.41]** Her objections were both idealistic (the company functioned like a family, and unionization would generate a division between employer and employees) and financial (the union would withhold dues from an already modest pay check).[163]

Union restrictions inhibited artistic experimentation. One area where this tension played out was flooring. In the 1960s and 1970s, when the company had very few theatrical bookings, Events were performed in public squares, gymnasia, armories, and amphitheatres, all of which threw up generative problems. In Piazza San Marco, Venice, in 1972, for example, the dancers were each equipped with a chair and a broom: they pushed the crowd back with the former before sweeping away the pigeon shit with the latter. They danced for a short period, then moved around the square, repeatedly pushing the chairs and sweeping, so that as many people as possible could see the work.

Such unsprung surfaces nevertheless strained the dancers' bodies. In a lecture-demonstration from 1969, Cunningham

161. "AGMA dancers achieve new three-year National Agreement," *AGMAZINE*, vol. xxxviii, no.1, December 1983, p.1. Cunningham dancers joined AGMA in 1968.

162. Letter to Hy Faine, AGMA, signed by dancers in seven modern dance companies, 28 January 1967. Merce Cunningham Dance Foundation Inc. Records, Additions, (S)*MGZMD 351, box 20, folder 5.

163. Prior to unionization, Brown writes, there was no assumption that one danced in order to earn money: "In the early fifties, no matter what modern-dance group one danced with, it was a privilege one paid for; paid for by outside work, any kind one could get that would allow time for daily classes and rehearsals and the infrequent performance. Rarely was anything paid beyond a token fee." Experimental dance, in her view, should be subsidized by dancers and choreographers "out of passion," rather than being the beneficiaries of funding from the NEA, NYSCA, Ford Foundation, Exxon, Philip Morris "or any other establishment Santa Claus." Brown, *Chance and Circumstance*, p.56. Her attitude reflects a youthful freedom from responsibilities: Brown notes that she and her partner (the composer Earle Brown) lived on $20 a week, he walked home 45 blocks from work, and their one big meal of the week was with John Cage's parents. Such a lifestyle is clearly not viable for anyone living with children, elderly parents, or illness.

Beverly

New York City, New York
January 28, 1967

Mr. Hy Faine
American Guild of Musical Artists
1841 Broadway
New York, New York

Dear Hy Faine:

We the members of the following companies listed are in common agreement that the current insistence of AGMA to unionize the modern dance companies is against our present interests and desires. And that any such unionization by AGMA would be contrary to the creative welfare of the modern dance field.

We wish to thank you for your concern.

Alvin Ailey Dance Co.

Judith Jamison
Alvin Harum
James Truitte
Thelma Hill
Jeri Edley

Merce Cunningham Dance Co.

Gus Solomons Jr.
Albert L. Reid Jr.
Beverly Emmons
Valda Setterfield
Peter Saul
Sandra Neels
Yseult Riopelle
Carolyn Brown

Erik Hawkins Dance Co.

on tour to May 10/67
Penelope Shaw
WAS TELEPHONED AND AGREES TO LETTER, AS A COMPANY.

Murray Louis Dance Co.

Raymond Johnson
Michael Podolski
Susan Buirge
Phyllis Lamhut
Wanda Pruska
Caroline Carlson
Bill Frank
Murray Louis

Paul Taylor Dance Co.

Sharon Kinney Bender for the Paul Taylor

COMPANY ON TOUR AGREES to LETTER AS A COMPANY.

Alvin Nikolais Dance Co.

Raymond Johnson
Michael Podolski
Dale Ominston
Susan Buirge
Phyllis Lamhut
Bill Frank
Wanda Pruska
Caroline Carlson
Murray Louis

Norman Walker Dance Co.

Norman Walker
Cora Cahan
Pamela Ladimer
Dale Best
Alice Gill
Gay Delanghe
Jo Anne Bruggeman
Ronnie Zakai
Marcia Wolfson
Jerry Grimes

Fig.41
Letter to AGMA opposing unionization, signed by dancers of seven modern dance companies, 1967.

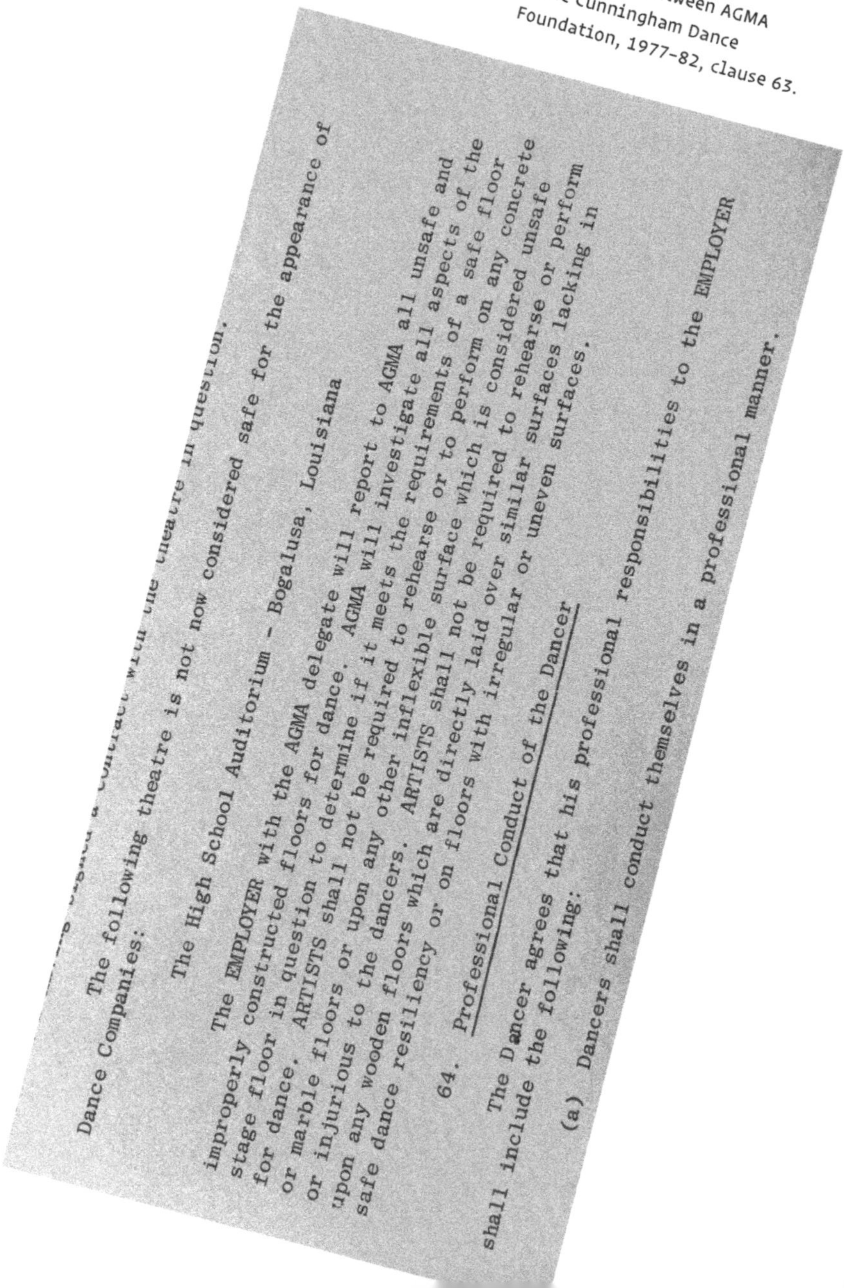

... signed a contract with the theatre in question.

The following theatre is not now considered safe for the appearance of Dance Companies:

The High School Auditorium - Bogalusa, Louisiana

The EMPLOYER with the AGMA delegate will report to AGMA all unsafe and improperly constructed floors for dance. AGMA will investigate all aspects of the stage floor in question to determine if it meets the requirements of a safe floor for dance. ARTISTS shall not be required to rehearse or to perform on any concrete or marble floors or upon any other inflexible surface which is considered unsafe or injurious to the dancers. ARTISTS shall not be required to rehearse or perform upon any wooden floors which are directly laid over similar surfaces lacking in safe dance resiliency or on floors with irregular or uneven surfaces.

64. Professional Conduct of the Dancer

The Dancer agrees that his professional responsibilities to the EMPLOYER shall include the following:

(a) Dancers shall conduct themselves in a professional manner.

Fig.42
Basic Agreement between AGMA and the Cunningham Dance Foundation, 1977–82, clause 63.

describes the recent Gymnasium Event #5 at SUNY New Paltz: "The space is handsome, but the floors are varnished and over cement. The back and the thighs ache for two days."[164] Dancers increasingly objected to the stress placed on their feet and ankles when performing in non-traditional spaces, and the expectation arose that all floors should be "sprung" (that is, able to absorb shock and thus support the dancer's muscles and joints). AGMA's Basic Agreement with the Cunningham Dance Foundation for the period 1977–1980 features a new clause regarding "unsafe theatres." **[Fig.42]** It specifies that "ARTISTS shall not be required to rehearse or to perform on any concrete or marble floors or upon any other inflexible surface which is considered unsafe or injurious to the dancers."[165] From this point on, the company no longer performed outdoors without specially installed flooring, and Events were staged in more conventional locations. The 1996–99 Agreement expanded the "unsafe theatres" clause specifically to reference "unusual public spaces as museums, in which the performing surface may be concrete, marble, or some other inflexible material."[166] Cunningham observed how floor surfaces have a direct relationship to movement. Since the invention of Marley (a type of vinyl floor), he noted in 1991, there are "more turns" and "more spins of varying forms" in his choreography, which simply wasn't possible earlier as "the floors were often so poor, it was difficult, almost impossible, to turn in barefeet."[167]

The reduction of risk was not just physical, but also mental. Event orders of the 1970s and 1980s had been issued to dancers on the day of the performance, keeping everyone on their literal and metaphoric toes. Their ability to perform excerpts out of

164. Lecture demonstration, Brooklyn Academy, 18 September 1969, in Merce Cunningham Dance Foundation Inc. Records, Additions, (S)*MGZMD 351, box 29, folder 4, Jerome Robbins Dance Division, NYPLPA.

165. Clause 63, Basic Agreement between AGMA and Cunningham Dance Foundation, 1977–1980, p.25, AGMA Archives, New York. Clause 63 continues: "ARTISTS shall not be required to rehearse or perform upon any wooden floors which are directly laid over similar surfaces lacking in safe dance resiliency or on floors with irregular or uneven surfaces."

166. Clause 63, Basic Agreement between AGMA and Cunningham Dance Foundation, 1996–99, pp.36–37, AGMA Archives, New York. This clause goes on to refer to two others, 23(j) and 27(g), both of which specify that "the ARTIST will not be penalized for refusal to rehearse and/or perform on a concrete or carpeted floor even though it may be covered in linoleum." Clause 27(g) rephrases this as follows: "After consultation with the EMPLOYER with best efforts to seek mutual remedies, ARTISTS shall not be penalized for refusal to rehearse on a concrete floor, even though it may have a linoleum covering." The fact that this is stated in three ways indicates the degree to which flooring had become a pressing issue.

167. Cunningham, "Cunningham Technique" lecture, 20 July 1991, Merce Cunningham Dance Foundation Inc. Records, Additions, (S)*MGZMD 351, box 30, folder 1.

sequence and in new contexts was tested, and thereby ensured that the dancers exuded a certain energy. In the 1960s and 70s, dancers would write the Event order on their arms with pen, which gradually rubbed off with sweat as the performance wore on.[168] They were responsible for calculating which side of the stage to exit in order to be on the correct side for the next entrance, and had to adapt to performing excerpts with different facings, and in new sequences, to completely different music. Numerous former dancers have described the excitement of this process, and how it constituted the most stimulating and "free" work they did with Cunningham.[169] The first two decades of the Events were a testimony both to the dancers' adaptability and the amount of trust Cunningham placed in them. Later members of the company found this spontaneity more stressful and preferred the rigor and reassurance of rehearsal. In 1993, dancer Chris Komar recalled how younger members of the company couldn't cope with the responsibility: "You know, they need to practice, practice, practice. This one girl had to practice just walking onstage and off again, like, four or five times [...] they even have to practice passing by each other. I mean, my God! You do this on the street all the time, passing by people!"[170]

With the development of the multi-stage Events in the 2000s, performances required weeks of careful preparation. Platform areas were mapped out in the studio and the transitions between them were meticulously rehearsed. Such performances demanded "a different level of virtuosity," recalls former dancer Rashaun Mitchell: dancers had to be aware of the timing not just on their own stage but also the one to which they were next headed, requiring new extensions of attention.[171] Even single-stage Events started to be rehearsed,

168. Valda Setterfield, interview with the author, New York, 14 March 2018; corroborated by dancer Alan Good in a comment to the author, New York, 25 January 2019.

169. Neil Greenberg recalls that Events "felt more truly like the Cunningham experiment—a destabilization of meaning. A repertory piece took on a 'meaning world', with its choreography, sets, sounds, and lighting. Yet the same piece could be totally destabilized in an Event." Interview with the author, 8 March 2018.

170. Komar continues: "What was so great about these early Events, and especially in the 70s—was the challenge, the spontaneousness of it and the unknown aspect of it. We didn't know—anything could happen. And it made it so much more exciting. And people dealt with it well. They dealt with the responsibility of getting into the space where they needed to be—and when they needed to be there. And now I find so many of the dancers can't cope, individually, with it." Komar, oral history interview, 15 November 1993, p.99, Jerome Robbins Dance Division, NYPLPA.

171. Rashaun Mitchell, interview with the author, via Skype, 30 March 2018. He continues: "running from one stage to the next, making sure you've completed this duet over here so that you can be over there on that other stage to do this other trio—and those timings were really a complex puzzle. [...] it's so challenging – just executing the movement that you're doing in the moment but also having to be aware of what that person is doing on that stage. You get to the point where you can look over and see someone doing another movement on another stage and know exactly where in time they are."

 as Cunningham grew increasingly uncomfortable with unpredictability as he aged.[172] The spontaneity of the early years, along with the adaptability of the dancers, became altogether more practiced, rehearsed, virtuosic—and professional. The Events became less about adaptability and more about "flexibility" in the neoliberal sense: the adaptation of oneself to a governing set of norms aimed at competitiveness, productivity, and professionalism.

This professionalization was of course intertwined with unionization, but also with expansion and financial stability. Art Becofsky, who worked his way up from office assistant to executive director between 1974 and 1994, increased the company's financial turnover from $260,00 a year to over a million within four years; he was also instrumental in obtaining large grants for new work from the National Endowment for the Arts, among other organizations. In a 1997 interview, he laments the difficulty of negotiating with AGMA, which always asked for increased pay at financially difficult moments, and in ways that he saw as irresponsible, cutting into the time available to make new work.[173] Yet this professionalization was equally the outcome of his own impressive efforts to stabilize the company financially and increase revenue. He goes on to bemoan the change in dancers hired by the company during the course of his twenty-year tenure. In the 1970s, dancers had diverse intellectual interests, and arrived with a college degree in literature or music; as the company became more successful and secured contracts and higher salaries, dancers came to perceive the company as a secure career option, rather than an aesthetic commitment. By the time Becofsky left in 1994, he pithily recalled, dancers could earn $40,000–$50,000 a year but were more interested in knowing the dental benefits than the rehearsal schedule.[174]

Yet it was obvious that the frugality of Carolyn Brown's generation, who waitressed and bartended in order to be part of an intoxicating avant-garde experiment, was no longer viable by the 1990s. And nor should it have been. By this point Cunningham himself was an institution. Risk was now commodified as endless novelty—a new combination of music and sets announced upfront, rather than an unknown problem that had to be overcome prior to (and during) the performance. The former can be calculated in advance, but the latter was a gamble that determined both what could be performed *and* the dancers' physical safety. By the late 1980s, if not earlier, Cunningham's Events had become a safe bet—their uniqueness was simply a rhetorical amplification of the contextual singularity that is constitutive of most live performance. The Event orders, meanwhile, had become more standardized, even formulaic, drawing on just a handful of repertory works that were subject to only slightly different recombination from evening to evening.[175]

172. Former Cunningham dancer Jennifer Goggans recalls that shortly after she joined the company in 2000, all Events began to be rehearsed. Seminar at Center for Ballet and the Arts, NYU, 23 April 2018.

173. Becofsky, oral history interview, 26 August 1997, pp.164–5, Jerome Robbins Dance Division, NYPLPA.

174. Becofsky, oral history interview, 26 August 1997, p.57, p.125, Jerome Robbins Dance Division, NYPLPA.

175. As early as 1989 the Event orders show decreasing variation from night to night. Cunningham's Event orders for the European tour of that year all begin with the “slow walk” or “slow movement” of *Scramble* and end with “fast dance” from *Scramble*; in between are positioned Cunningham's own solos (*Chair Dance*, *Loops*, *50 Looks*) and excerpts drawn from just the following works: *Roaratorio*, *Aeon*, *Trails*, *Un Jour ou Deux*, *Canfield*, *Torse*, *Signals*, and *Changing Steps*.

Criteria

Cunningham often stated that Events "allowed not for an evening of dances so much as an experience of dance." This quotation appears on every Event program, translated into the language of the country where the performance is being held. What this somewhat cryptic claim suggests is a prioritization of ephemeral presence and immediacy, rather than densely layered artistic signification. It implies that choreography can be stripped of its original supporting components (costumes, décor, music), be put into juxtaposition with new ones, and still hold its integrity as dance. As dancer Neil Greenberg helpfully explains, "In Events you see the *dancing* much more, because [...] a human dancing becomes the meaning."[176] An "experience of dance" thus denotes the audience's consumption of pure movement sequences independent of the formal structure of "a work."

This ontological slipperiness of dancing without a work has had ramifications for the Events' critical reception. *New York Times* dance critic Jack Anderson, for example, argued that the Events were impregnable to conventional critical analysis because no two Events were the same, and thus no stable criterion of judgment could be applied.[177] This position is reiterated in press coverage throughout the 1970s and 1980s, where critics express frustration that the Events can't be analyzed in terms of a

176. Greenberg, interview with the author, New York, 8 March 2018.

177. Jack Anderson, "Dances about Everything and Dances about Some Things" (1976). See also Clive Barnes in the *New York Times*, 3 December 1975, p.35, who implies that the Events are not "proper dances."

unified work. The trio from *Torse* can't be judged as *Torse*, or the Jigs from *Roaratorio* as *Roaratorio*, because they are incomplete fragments—presented without the costumes, lighting, or music of the repertory productions. The implication is that Cunningham's choreography is impoverished and undecidable when it appears without its supporting world.

Yet Cunningham had always asserted the independence of choreography from set design, music, and costumes. The Events demonstrate the degree to which these other components were not just non-integral but ultimately *removable*. The core of his practice was the choreography, which had its own integrity and rhythm regardless of context. In other words, the experience of his practice was never the totality of music-décor-lighting-costumes-choreography, but the immediate perceptual experience of virtuosic bodily movement in the moment. Rather than offering a depth model of the work of art (i.e., a stable entity that can be subjected to repeated viewings and analysis), the Events underscore Cunningham's understanding of dance as unfixable flow, presence, and ephemerality.

However, this reading of the Events as somehow *outside* or *beyond* a "work" is insufficient. In most modern and contemporary art forms, it is hard to imagine creativity without its larger framing: e.g., poetry without a poem, an action without its context, or art without an object, however ephemeral.[178] In the case of the Events, however, this frame is the conceptual structure, beginning with a primary set of requirements that Cunningham printed on all Event programs: "Presented without intermission, these Events consist of complete dances, excerpts of dances from the repertory, and often new sequences arranged for the particular performance and place." Alongside this definition exists a second level of less explicit parameters concerning duration (approximately ninety minutes), costumes (always unitards), and, in the later years at least, décor (large enough to hold its own on stage). Finally, a hidden third level of internal choreographic structure, discussed above, is put in place: a striking opening; variations of large and small groups of dancers;

178. Lydia Goehr has persuasively argued for the emergence of the "work-concept" in music around 1800, when attention shifted away from a functional view of performance to the idea of an autonomous work of art. Accordingly, this changed the expectations and ideals by which musicians thought about their compositions, and scores became regulative and proprietory. Goehr, *The Imaginary Museum of Musical Works: An Essay in the Philosophy of Music*, Oxford University Press, 2007 (revised edition), especially chapter 7.

fast and slow excerpts; two or three Cunningham solos positioned at key moments; a group finale.

The structure of the Events thus generates a *dispositif* that can be filled with endlessly remixed content, in the manner of the database model proposed by Piekut to describe the musical performances accompanying the Events in the 1970s. (This is not the case with Cunningham's other innovation, the VideoDance, which only exists in the form of individual works.) For Cunningham, the Events were a "work," albeit one that changed continually over the course of their forty-five-year existence.[179] They are, however, best thought of as both a work *and* a format, and in this lies their originality. It's also what produces the difficulty of judging what makes a "good" Event, because the container remains constant while the contents always vary. A good Event is arguably a matter of energy: a fortuitous synergy between the performers, the choice of excerpts, the location, the décor (if any), the music—and even the presence of the audience. It's a "rendez-vous" (to invoke Carrie Noland's Duchampian reading of Cunningham)—a set of relationships that simply takes off or ignites.[180] Like a good party, the magic dissipates quickly and can't be captured in photographs. The most reproduced Event images tend to be those in striking locations where the site becomes an extraordinary set that dominates all the other elements: Persepolis and Venice (1972), Grand Central Terminal (1987), Tate Modern (2003) and Dia Beacon (2007–09).

179. Events have been performed after Cunningham's death, such as the final performances of the Legacy Tour at the Park Avenue Armory in 2011. These have a different character to those arranged by Cunningham; former dancers have variously described them to me as "more pedagogic" (in that they dutifully represent the work of different decades) and "more greatest hits" (in that they don't allow for periods of creative boredom).

180. Carrie Noland uses Marcel Duchamp's term "rendez-vous" (which the French artist used to describe the ready-made) to account for Cunningham's production of relationality from non-relation: "Throughout his career, he conceived of his dances as encounters or meetings, opportunities for couplings that rarely unfold into plots. The rendez-vous was for him a point of departure, not just for the ready-made—the neutral movement-content he placed in his gamut—but also, and more frequently, for the human scenarios that the chance-chosen movement content... could suggest." Noland, *Merce Cunningham: After the Arbitrary*, p.38.

The Events' iterability and (at least partial) site-specificity are characteristics shared with avant-garde art of the early 1960s. Both tend towards the anti-expressive, modular, neutral, collaborative, and context dependent. Even the name "Event" conforms to ideas in the air at that time—evoking the concision of the Fluxus "event score" as well as the non-specific immediacy of something simply "happening." The protagonists of these tendencies—George Brecht (event scores) and Allan Kaprow (happenings)—had both attended Cage's summer class at the New School in 1958, which sought to redefine music as "events in sound-space," thereby expanding traditional tonality to the inclusion in a score of anything that happens.[181] Other artists who adopted the term include La Monte Young (compositions focused on the "singular event," 1960), Yoko Ono (*Flower Event*, 1962–3), Mieko Shiomi (*Event for Midnight*, 1963), Carolee Schneemann (*Newspaper Event* at Judson, 1963), and Takehisa Kosugi (event scores, 1964–5). Cage's *Theatre Piece no.1*, often referred to as the first happening, was also called *The Event* or *Untitled Event*. In each instance, the event was a deceptively capacious vessel into which a disparate array of content could be poured. Cunningham's adoption of this term in 1964 thus tied him to a younger generation of intermedial innovators associated with Fluxus, Judson and experimental music, even while he also rejected key aspects of this work—its brevity, exuberance, indeterminacy, and above all deskilling.[182] Cunningham's Events have a carefully structured format and consistency of execution, unlike the everyday aesthetic and improvisatory spirit of the younger generation's approach. The fact that Cunningham had to develop his own training method for the dancers in his company is just one indication of his deep attachment to virtuosity.

181. Event scores were used widely by a younger generation of artists and musicians in Cage's circle, and comprise short written instructions for performance. They are indeterminate in the sense that decisions about how to interpret and perform them are left open to the viewer/reader/participant. Happenings refer to both to artist's theatre and more participatory events, both of which were held in downtown loft spaces and occasionally galleries. See Liz Kotz, "Post-Cagean Aesthetics and the 'Event' Score," *October* no. 95, Winter 2001, pp.54–89, and Allan Kaprow, *Assemblage, Environments, and Happenings*, NY: H.N. Abrams, 1966.

182. For deskilling, see Ken Friedman, "Getting into Events," in Friedman (ed.), *Fluxus Performance Workbook*, Trondheim, 1990: El Djarida.

The tone of Cunningham's Events was distinctively different to contemporaneous work at Judson, and seem to have had little of the lightness and humour of his earlier works like *Dime a Dance* (1953) and *Antic Meet*, which included references to vaudeville. After *Story*, Cunningham's aesthetic register was increasingly cool and objective, leading art historian Moira Roth to describe it as "indifferent," apolitical and ironic.[183] She positions the conscious neutrality of Cunningham and his circle as an aesthetic rejection of high modernist psychology and emoting (be this the mytho-ritual of Martha Graham or the masculinist bombast of Abstract Expressionist painting) and as a pragmatic political response to Senator McCarthy's blacklisting

183. Roth, "The Aesthetic of Indifference," p.48.

of leftist sympathizers. Her article overstates the case: it's not that Cunningham and Cage repress their politics, but that they are deeply invested in freedom as a perceptual act. Cunningham connected life in a democratic society—which he understood as coexistence unfettered by relationships of hierarchy and oppression—to his aesthetic investment in independence: the self-sufficiency of choreography (from music, from narrative, from décor, from lighting, from costumes); the autonomy of the dancers (from each other, from the choreographer, from the audience, and from any representation of social relationships); and the non-relatedness of the body (whose parts are increasingly separated and accorded movements as disconnected units).[184] At times, this comes close to rugged individualism and, ironically, is the same freedom that was being promoted as quintessentially American in post-war CIA-sponsored exhibitions of Abstract Expressionism. As Cunningham discovered on his tour to South America in 1968 and to Eastern Europe in 1972, his choreographic abstraction was interpreted by the authorities as Western propaganda.[185]

Independence and autonomy also characterize the position of the viewer. Dance historian Susan Leigh Foster speculates that Cunningham's deflection of meaning away from himself and onto the individual response of the audience was a way to find "protection for his homosexual identity."[186] As a result, she argues, his approach to choreography constructed a new role for the viewer—one that emphasizes the audience's singular response, rather than sharing in a collective experience of meaning.[187] In this, Cunningham was entirely in tune with contemporaneous US artists, including some of his collaborators, who refused to explain their work in terms of inner meaning—think of Frank Stella's claim that "what you see is what you see." This aversion to interpretation can be seen in Cunningham's short but revealing interview with Arlene Croce, in which he offers the following mocking response to her inquiry as to whether

184. See Cunningham, Lecture notes for *A Method of Making Dances*, Roslyn Arts Center, Long Island, 4/17/57, p.4, in Merce Cunningham Dance Foundation Inc. Records, Additions, (S)*MGZMD 351, box 29, folder 1. This is is as optimistic and liberal as Cage's desire to make music as "a way of waking up to the very life we're living which is so excellent once one gets one's mind and one's desire out of one's way." John Cage, "Experimental Music," in *Silence*, p.12.

185. See Gordon Mumma's comments on the Cunningham tours of 1968 and 1972 in Mumma, *Cybersonic Arts: Adventures in American New Music*, University of Illinois Press, 2015, p.135.

186. Susan Leigh Foster, "Closets Full of Dances: Modern Dance's Performance of Masculinity and Sexuality," pp.173–4.

187. "Because the dance rebuffed all efforts to find narrative continuity, it created neither storytellers nor listeners. Adamantly, it said nothing but did something." Foster, "Closets Full of Dances," p.173.

Winterbranch is about nuclear war. He draws on the different responses he overheard on the 1964 world tour:

> *Winterbranch*: a) bombed cities – New York; b) concentration camps – Germany; c) nuclear war – Japan; d) shipwreck (my favourite. From a sea-captain's wife). Right you are if you think you are.[188]

By refusing to articulate any specific meaning for his works, Cunningham rendered them blank screens of projection for the viewer's own preoccupations. Former dancer Douglas Dunn recalls:

188. Cunningham, in Arlene Croce, "An Interview with Merce Cunningham," *Ballet Review* vol.1, no.4, 1966, p.4.

> In Pittsburgh [1970] we performed in a student center, modern architecture, with a very long space in the middle, and on either side were big loungers with rugs and couches—it was a student center where people came and hung out. And we danced on a wooden part in the middle. It was a long Event and afterwards there was a talk, I can't remember if it was formalized or not, but I remember it because of the responses. There were two main themes, according to those watching: drug addiction, and the Vietnam War. This was one of those moments where you realize that if you don't tell people what to think about your work, they'll think whatever the hell they want.[189]

The idea that a Cunningham Event could thematize drug addiction and US intervention in Vietnam today seems delightfully outrageous, so entrenched is our understanding of his work as non-representational.[190] Cunningham's silence was thus strategic, enabling him to tread a careful line at a time when his younger peers were making more explicitly protest-based work about those very subjects—such as Rainer's version of *Trio A* performed naked, with the stars and stripes draped around the dancers' necks, at "The People's Flag Show" in 1970.[191]

For Cunningham, like so many white male artists of the 1950s and 60s, politics was

189. Douglas Dunn, interview with the author, New York, 11 April 2018.

190. Powerful arguments have been made against this received idea, perhaps most strikingly by Callahan in "The Gay Divorce of Dance and Music."

191. Ikegami asserts that Cunningham's sociopolitical neutrality was the reason for his accessibility to audiences across many cultures, and optimistically concludes that because of this, the Events are a "truly global format." Hiroko Ikegami, "A medium for engagement: on the Merce Cunningham Dance Company's Events," in Fionne Meade and Joan Rothfuss (eds.), *Merce Cunningham: Common Time*, Minneapolis : Walker Art Center, 2017, p.84.

primarily a question of form: spatial relationships as metaphor, dehierarchized and detached from any type of engagement with social content, social conflict, or for that matter, social unity. Standardized unitards served to nullify gender and racial difference, even while partnering and gender dynamics remained traditional: men lift women, and there are no same-sex duets.[192] The white body reads as "blank" in a way that a non-white body does not; for many artists, the luxury of exploring a neutral aesthetic with an unmarked body was never an option.[193] In this, Cunningham's aesthetic of indifference is typically mid-century white male American: minimal expression, a no-nonsense modularity, collaboration as tacitly agreed appropriateness, and an interpretive schema open enough to accommodate whatever the viewer wishes to project upon it. At the same time, Cunningham could be said to queer this set of clichés—especially in the 1950s and 60s—with fleeting interruptions of vaudeville and Dada: bicycles, houseplants, champagne and cigarettes, and (thanks to Rauschenberg) dresses made of parachutes. From the 1970s on, the formalism of his choreography was more in tune with broader aesthetic tendencies in U.S. art that assert depersonalization and reject European aesthetics as hierarchical and burdensomely metaphysical.[194] Throughout his work, compositional neutrality worked simultaneously to open up and close down (and to closet) interpretation.

192. For a rare critique of gender dynamics in Cunningham, see Jill Johnston, "Jigs, Japes, and Joyce," *Art in America*, January 1987, p.105. Cunningham's chance procedures "never generated a male-male duet until 1993," the year after Cage died, observes Susan Manning in *Modern Dance, Negro Dance: Race in Motion*, Minneapolis: University of Minnesota Press, 2004, p.208.

193. Mannning notes that Cunningham presented dancers as "distinct yet interchangeable personae... [who] could not be reduced to gendered, sexualized, or racialized identities, yet Cunningham's choreography still created a closet for the gay male dancer and relied upon the generalizing power of whiteness. Not until 1965 did Cunningham add a dancer of colour to his previously Euro-American ensemble." Manning, *Modern Dance, Negro Dance*, p.208.

194. See for example Donald Judd, "Specific Objects," *Arts Yearbook* 8, 1965, pp.74–82.

Closing

Positioned between classical and avant-garde, modern and post-modern, Cunningham's choreography managed to be transitional for six decades. At each point we find his practice facing, Janus-like, in two directions: backwards to modernism, and forwards to contemporary dance. If this middle ground seemed to calcify over the decades, then the Events are its best index. A format so convenient that it was performed more frequently than any single repertory work, the Events were above all a practical solution to a slew of doggedly material problems—the institutional and infrastructural realities of running a company. They were a way to show Cunningham's work in non-traditional venues at a time when US theatres ignored him; a process to deal with the too-rapid turnover of company members, especially in the early 1970s; a strategy to give dancers enough performance dates to claim benefits; a means to tour internationally on the cheap, without having to ship crates of décor; a method for keeping past repertory alive in the bodies of younger company members; an excuse to collaborate with young artists and musicians, and thus to present ongoing stimuli for the choreographer.

The Events' transitionality nevertheless accomplished important shifts in the idea of a work of art, and pressure many of the keywords of late twentieth-century art: collaboration, curation, spectatorship, composition. Events helped to shift the concept of art from a depth model (a rich and repeatable "work") to a continually shifting, recombinatory "format" with endlessly variable content. Cunningham could thus produce an infinity of "new and unique" evenings of dance, highly marketable to institutions, even while nothing substantially new was ever performed. Manifestos of non-narrative recombination, the Events dismantle Cunningham's repertoire even while they adhere to traditional theatrical conventions of unity, variety, and contrast. They deploy a database structure of possibilities, but the "gamut" remains tied to Cunningham's own output, rather than embracing the heterogeneity of other dance compositions or traditions.

Although the Events deploy a multi-media logic—collaborating with musicians, artists, and designers—ultimately these components are dispensable, and the core of the work is the medium-specific purity of choreography, "the experience of dance itself." They articulate a model of collaboration that thrusts the contemporary romanticization of this concept into disarray: no longer a model of profound exchange but of parallel play that only worked as long as everybody tacitly agreed with each other.

The mid-1960s embrace of television as liveness supplies the Events' model of duration, and gives rise to an understanding of spectatorship as one of choosing channels. The Events thus provide an alternative to dominant accounts of "passive" televisual and theatrical spectatorship by foregrounding eyeshift as a mode of live editing by each individual viewer.

Contingency and risk—including the risk of physical injury—were central to the innovative energy of the Events in the 1960s and 1970s. Following unionization, these were increasingly constrained, leading to new levels of responsibility (to dancers, to venues, to donors) and thus to artistic caution.

Whatever criteria we bring to Cunningham's work today is, of course, more or less moot now that it has become canonical. The legacy of the Events can be seen in the many different solutions for programming dance in museums through the 2010s. It can be found in works that function equally well onstage or in galleries, such as Belgian choreographer Anne Teresa de Keersmaeker reinventing her stage production *Vortex Temporum* (2013) as the touring exhibition "Work/Travail/Arbeid" (2015). It's present in the invention of formats that can be filled with different content for each iteration and yet remain an identifiable "work," as in *Expo-zéro* (2009–) and *20 Dancers for the XX Century* (2012–) by the French choreographer Boris Charmatz; like Cunningham's Events, these works remain authored and unavailable for adoption by other choreographers. It can be found in compositional structures that allow artists to recycle their existing work in new configurations: another French choreographer, Xavier Le Roy, has recycled his back catalogue of solos in a performance exhibition called *"Retrospective"* (2012–), performed by dancers local to the city where it is being shown. Trajal Harrell's *Friend of a Friend* (2021), to name a further example, comprised a two-hour loop of highlights of his recent works, presented three times over the course of one evening in the galleries of Fondation Cartier; Harrell explicitly acknowledges Cunningham's Events as a point of reference.

Perhaps more importantly, Cunningham's invention of a format has become a blueprint for experiments that allow choreographers to reach new and bigger audiences beyond the theatre. After wading through his archive at the Library for the Performing Arts, I am left with the overriding impression of Cunningham as an artist who wanted at all costs for his work to be seen. The context might be fruitful, or it might not. For a visual art audience, this interest in probing new spaces has enduring appeal— as does the pleasure of virtuosity after so many decades of de-skilled and anti-virtuosic visual art performance. The sheer beauty of honed young bodies moving exquisitely in space, unencumbered by objecthood and market value, can be irresistible. In the pleasurable specificity of each performer's body—seen so much more clearly in the proximity of the gallery than onstage—we find that we no longer have to choose between authorship and indeterminacy, agency and chance, plenitude and emptiness, expression or control. Cunningham offers us the opportunity to find one at work within the other, and against the other—or, as Carrie Noland has argued, one *after* the other: expression *after* its purging, relationships *after* their dismantling, individuality *after* its suppression.

One might also add creativity despite its privatization. The arc of Cunningham's company, and the role of Events within it, show the effort and ingenuity required to survive and thrive as a choreographer in late twentieth-century America. Here, the script for success is always predicated on expansion: more grants, more dances, more shows, more income, more dancers, more reviews, more pressure. Balancing these imperatives with creative integrity is the tightrope act that choreographers must navigate if they are to work in a country where the survival of culture depends on the unreliable generosity of private individuals.

Fig.43
Page of notes showing Cunningham's timings for *Scramble*, *Canfield*, *Fractions*, *Numbers*, *10s with Shoes*, *Torse*, etc., 12 March 1983. Merce Cunningham Dance Company Choreographic Records, (S) *MGZMD 295, box 12, folder 5.

Scramble

Sl. knots - 2'15
Sl. trio - 6'45
2 men - 7'15
Lunges - 8'00
Huddle - 9'25
3 men - 11'40
CHK - 13'25
Fall/leap - 13'45
Duet - 16'30
Lift - 19'15
CK - 21'45
Foot Dance - 23'05
Sl. walk - 24'30
[IV|21|P3]

CF

CC. 6'45
Duet 6'10

Duet #7 2'20
◇ 1'10
Qu #7 2'30
Xings 1'20
Duet #2 2'25
Shoulder 0'45
Qu #2 2'30
Ships 1'30 [14'20]

ER ① 6'00
② 6'00

#'s - 5'45

Trials - 2'00

10's - 15'00

Torque - 1'15 - Prog
5'30 - Trio
10'00 3'15 End

Ste Trio. 2'45
Q5. 5'45
8'30

CLST 42.00
C.C. order

M Solo 3'00
Oh Solo 3'00
50 Looks 8'00
Loops ; Rands 2'00
chairwaist 5'45

Figs 2'00

E/P Duet 3'15

III|12|P3
Trails
1. 2'35
2. 4.50
3. 8'15
4. 10'55 to Duet
5. 14'25 "
6. 18'45 entrance
7. 19'55 Duet
8. 21'45
9. 25'20

Q4 17'00

CH|FN [15'00]
1.
2. 5'45
3. 10.55
4. 14.00
5. 17.15
6. 22.00 [Arg]
7. 24'30 [Duets]
8. 28'00

Locale
1. 4'00
2. 14'03
3. 23'30
4. 28'20

Acknowledgements

A casual conversation with Jonah Bokaer at NYU's Center for Ballet and the Arts (CBA) kick-started this project; thank you Jonah for your candour. The CBA went on to be a crucial incubator for this project, providing a space to work, a relationship with the Merce Cunningham Trust, and multiple opportunities to test out this material on inspiring colleagues. Huge thanks to Jennifer Homans and Andrea Salvatore.

The Merce Cunningham Trust has been nothing less than exceptional throughout this research: granting me access to the dance capsules and answering a million detailed questions. It's rare to encounter an artist's estate so generous and open-minded. I am enormously grateful to Ken Tabachnik and his team: the wonderful Nancy Dalva (the Trust's scholar-in-residence), Patricia Lent, Jennifer Goggans, and Shannon Resser.

Many former MCDC dancers and company members gave their precious time to answer my questions at a formative stage of my research, when I was still fumbling my way through this material: Charles Atlas, Douglas Dunn, Jennifer Goggans and Patricia Lent (again), Rashaun Mitchell, Silas Riener, Davison Scandrett, and the much-missed Valda Setterfield. A special thank you to Trevor Carlson and Neil Greenberg for their generous time and insights.

The Jerome Robbins Dance Division at the Library for the Performing Arts at New York Public Library has been an incredible resource. I spent many many happy hours trawling through the archives in 2018 thanks to a Dance Division Fellowship that fall. Special thanks to Linda Murray and Tanisha Jones for their ongoing support.

The good energy that exudes from the Cunningham Trust is, perhaps unsurprisingly, matched by that at the Rauschenberg Foundation, which offered me a research residency in Captiva during summer 2019. I spent a blissful month reading and writing in Bob's Main Studio; thank you Ralph Lemon for this connection.

Thank you to all the photographers who gave me permission to reproduce their beautiful images, often with low or no fees—most of all, James Klosty.

Three intellectual fellow-travellers have accompanied me on this research: David Grubbs, with whom I co-taught a *Cage and Cunningham* seminar at the Graduate Center in fall 2019, and from whom I learnt so much; Julia Robinson, who answered a slew of small questions and queries at random hours of day and night; and Benjamin Piekut, who heard various drafts and made great suggestions. Thank you all three. Other colleagues provided feedback on early drafts and helped bounce around ideas: Julia Bryan-Wilson, Lindsay Caplan, Carrie Lambert-Beatty, and Jonah Westerman.

Many thanks to Nick Mauss and Ken Okishii for creative brainstorming about how to handle images, design, and the dance/art relationship in book form. Our conversations helped me work with Matthew Young, this book's designer, who was a wonderful collaborator. His design is adapted from Cunningham's 1968 book *Changes: Notes on Choreography*.

Many graduate students contributed to this project, including all those in the *Cage and Cunningham* class. Rachel Valinsky trawled through the Cunningham archives for me, as did Flora Brandl, who also provided translations and detailed feedback. Chiara Mannarino helped with picture research at a critical moment.

Nikki Columbus gave this a much-needed editorial pummelling for which I am eternally grateful. You think it's the dullest thing I have ever written, but you're my favourite person to dance with, so I'm dedicating it to you.

Photographic credits:

All photographs courtesy of Merce Cunningham Trust unless otherwise indicated.
Figs 4, 6, 8, 9, 15, 22, 23, 24, 25, 26, 27, 28, 41, 43: Courtesy of Merce Cunningham Trust and the Jerome Robbins Dance Division, Library for the Performing Arts, New York Public Library
Fig.3: Courtesy of Österreichische Nationalbibliothek, Vienna
Fig.11: Courtesy of Corbis via Getty Images
Fig.12: Courtesy of Shirley Streshinsky via the The Bancroft Library University of California, Berkeley
Fig.16: Courtesy of Alamy, Inc.
Fig.29: © 2022 Estate of Pablo Picasso / Artists Rights Society (ARS), New York
Fig.30: © 2022 Robert Rauschenberg Foundation / Licensed by VAGA at Artists Rights Society (ARS), NY
Fig.33: Courtesy of WNET Television
Fig.42: Courtesy of American Guild of Musical Artists

Design: Matthew Young, Young Studio (Cover: probsteibooks, Köln)
Editing: Nikki Columbus
Cover image: Event rehearsal, Théâtre Experimental, Fondation Maeght, Saint-Paul-de Vence, July 1970. Photo: James Klosty.

First published by
Verlag der Buchhandlung Walther und Franz König, Köln

Printed in Germany

ISBN 978-3-7533-0716-9

Distribution in Germany & Europe
Buchhandlung Walther und Franz König, Köln
Ehrenstr. 4, 50672 Köln
Tel +49 (0) 221/205 96 53 Fax +49 (0) 221/205 96 60
verlag@buchhandlung-walther-koenig.de

UK & Eire: *Cornerhouse Publications*
70 Oxford Street, Manchester M1 5NH, Great Britain
Tel +44 (0) 161 200 15 03 Fax +44 (0) 161 200 15 04
publications@cornerhouse.org

Outside Europe: *D.A.P.*
Distributed Art Publishers, Inc.
155 6th Avenue, 2nd Floor, New York, NY 10013, USA
Tel +1 (0) 212 627 1999 Fax +1 (0) 212 627 9484
eleshowitz@dapinc.com